STRATEGIC PLANNING AND IMPLEMENTATION
FOR ISLAMIC ORGANIZATIONS

STRATEGIC PLANNING AND IMPLEMENTATION FOR ISLAMIC ORGANIZATIONS

RAFIK ISSA BEEKUN

1401AH—1981AC

THE INTERNATIONAL INSTITUTE OF ISLAMIC THOUGHT
WASHINGTON • LONDON

© The International Institute of Islamic Thought, 1427 AH/2006 CE

The International Institute of Islamic Thought
P.O. Box 669, Herndon, VA 20172, USA

London Office
P.O. Box 126, Richmond, Surrey TW9 2UD, UK

This book is in copyright. Subject to statutory exception
and to the provisions of relevant collective licensing agreements,
no reproduction of any part may take place without
the written permission of the publishers.

ISBN 1-56564-064-0

In the Name of God,
the Most Gracious, the Most Merciful.

This book is dedicated to:
Dada Fowdar
and
Bhai Ahmed Atchia,
My early teachers of Islam,
and to
Muhib Durrani and Mohamed M. Saad,
my lifelong friends

Quotable Quotes

Allah[1] loves, when one of you is doing something, that he [or she] does it in the most excellent manner.

— Prophet Muhammad (p)[2]

A journey of a thousand miles must begin with a single step.

— Chinese proverb, Lao Tzu

You've got to come up with a plan. You can't wish things will get better.[3]

— Jack Welch, General Electric

Ibn Abbas (*ra*)[4] reported that when Allah's Messenger was asked about the major sins, he replied: "Associating partners with Allah (*swt*)[5] (*shirk*), despairing of Allah's Mercy, and believing that one is safe from Allah's Plan."

Not a single dawn breaks out without two angels calling out: "O Son of Adam! I am a new day and I witness your actions, so make the best out of me because I will never come back until the Day of Judgment.[6]"

— Prophet Muhammad

Table of Contents

Preface xi

Chapter 1
WHAT IS STRATEGIC MANAGEMENT? 1

Chapter 2
PRE-PLANNING 15

Chapter 3
SWOT ANALYSIS 25

Chapter 4
DEVELOPING VISION AND MISSION STATEMENTS 41

Chapter 5
IDENTIFYING AND PRIORITIZING GOALS 59

Chapter 6
GAP ANALYSIS 63

Chapter 7
CRAFTING STRATEGIES 65

Chapter 8
DEVELOPING MEASURABLE OBJECTIVES 75

Chapter 9
DEVELOPING OPERATIONAL PLANS 81

Chapter 10
DEVELOPING CONTINGENCY PLANS 87

Chapter 11
IMPLEMENTING THE STRATEGIC PLAN:
STRATEGY-LEADERSHIP FIT 95

Chapter 12
IMPLEMENTING THE STRATEGIC PLAN:
STRATEGY-STRUCTURE FIT 105

Chapter 13
IMPLEMENTING THE STRATEGIC PLAN:
THE STRATEGY-CULTURE FIT 117

Chapter 14
PERFORMANCE EVALUATION AND REVIEW 129

Chapter 15
THE CYCLE BEGINS AGAIN 141

Chapter 16
STRATEGY AND ETHICS 143

Chapter 17
TAWAKKUL OR TRUSTING IN ALLAH 153

Final Words 161

Appendix
    A. Strategic Planning and Implementation Worksheets 163
    B. Sample Strategic Plans and Case Examples 177
    C. Glossary of Islamic Terms 185

Endnotes 189

Bibliography 199

Index 205

Preface

There is a saying that "organizations don't plan to fail; they just fail to plan." Many Islamic organizations and businesses are known for their lack of planning and their inconsistent, short-term focus. Were they to examine closely Prophet Muhammad's *sirah* (the study of the life of the Prophet), they would realize that he understood and used strategy throughout his life. Having taught, researched, and consulted in strategy for almost two decades, I am addressing this book to you, as a Muslim leader, board member, or businessperson. Insha' Allah, this book will help you think and act proactively. The strategic planning and implementation process described here can be used in the context of any Islamic organization, whether it is for-profit or not-for-profit, a business, an Islamic center, or a mosque. While this book specifically targets Islamic organizations, namely any organization run by Muslims in accordance to Islamic principles. I have also used the material in this book to help out people of other faith-based communities in their own strategic planning. Good work to serve the Creator and to help fellow human beings should be as effective as possible.

I would like to acknowledge the contributions of Dr. Ahmad Sakr, Rushdi Siddiqui (director, Dow Jones Islamic Index), Rafi-uddin Shikoh (editor, www.dinarstandard.com [a global Islamic business website]), and Dr. Iqbal Unus (International Institute of Islamic Thought [IIIT]). Dr. Jamal Barzinji (chairman, IIIT) gently advised and coaxed me to finish this project. At IIIT, Jay Willoughby, my longstanding editor, patiently read through and subjected my work to his incisive yet helpful critical scrutiny. I also thank the many Islamic organizations and businesses across many countries and several continents that allowed me to work with them and to refine the subject matter gathered over almost a decade: specifically, Manzoor Ghori (chairman, Indian Muslim Relief and Charities), Dr. Faroque Khan (president, Islamic Center of Long Island), and Nihad Awad (executive director, Council of American Islamic Relations) have been joint collaborators in some of the successful strategic plans I have included as examples in this book. Finally, I want to thank my wife Nadiah, whose constancy, patience, and special understanding of my needs have always made it possible for me to achieve beyond my meager capabilities by the Grace of Allah.

Years ago, when I was a teenager growing up in Rose-Hill, Mauritius, two life-long students of Islam, Dada Fowdar and his friend Bhai Ahmed Atchia, took the time to discuss Islam with me and to teach me how to appreciate Allah's infinite wisdom and perfect logic. Muhib Durrani and Mohamed Saad, my role models and friends, have since inspired me to serve my Creator and Sustainer, Allah. I am in their debt eternally, and so dedicate this book to them.

I accept responsibility for any mistake in this book. Any good in this book is from Allah; any mistake is mine. Please e-mail me at rib19@columbia.edu with your feedback or write to me at the address given below. Allah the Almighty knows best. *Subhana Rabbi wa bihamdihi* (Glorified is my Lord with all praise due to Him).

Rafik I. Beekun
Managerial Sciences Department, MS 28
College of Business Administration
University of Nevada, Reno, NV, 89557-0206, USA
13 Rajab 1427 AH / 7 August 2006

Notice to Readers

Since this book is aimed both at for-profit and not-for-profit Islamic organizations, you may find some topics less appropriate for your organization than others. Please feel free to skip over these. If you are unsure, please e-mail the author, at rib19@columbia.edu, a brief message describing your organization, and he will let you know whether you are skipping any important part. In general, however, most of the techniques described in this book apply equally well to both types of Islamic organizations.

CHAPTER 1

WHAT IS STRATEGIC MANAGEMENT?

كُنتُمْ خَيْرَ أُمَّةٍ أُخْرِجَتْ لِلنَّاسِ تَأْمُرُونَ بِٱلْمَعْرُوفِ وَتَنْهَوْنَ عَنِ ٱلْمُنكَرِ وَتُؤْمِنُونَ بِٱللَّهِ ۗ وَلَوْ ءَامَنَ أَهْلُ ٱلْكِتَٰبِ لَكَانَ خَيْرًا لَّهُم ۚ مِّنْهُمُ ٱلْمُؤْمِنُونَ وَأَكْثَرُهُمُ ٱلْفَٰسِقُونَ ۝

You are the best of peoples, evolved for mankind, enjoining what is right, forbidding what is wrong, and believing in Allah. If only the People of the Book had faith, it were best for them: among them are some who have faith, but most of them are perverted transgressors. (Qur'an, 3:110)

Is strategic planning Islamic, or is it *bidah* (an innovation)?

Y ou know your Islamic organization needs to develop a clear strategy. You know there is no clear direction in what your mosque or Islamic institution does. You have suggested that your organization rethink what it is doing. Others ask if strategic planning is Islamic at all, or if it is *bidah* (an innovation)? As you ponder over this question, you recall some facts.

1
WHAT IS STRATEGIC MANAGEMENT?

Strategic Planning in the Bible, the Qur'an, and the *Sirah*

Even before the Qur'an was revealed,[1] we find Biblical support for strategic planning.[2] Moses (as),[3] a consummate strategist who led the nation of Israel out of Egypt, grappled with his role as leader. His father-in-law Jethro (Shu`ayb) understood his plight and taught him strategic human resource planning, namely, how to manage his work by delegating parts of it according to a well-established hierarchy. In the Bible, each of Israel's twelve tribes had separate areas in the camp, their own leaders, and specific responsibilities. Each tribe dealt with the day-to-day issues, while Moses focused on getting them to their overall goal.

Prophet David was a superb strategic thinker who understood strategy even while still a youth. For example, he did not attack Goliath's strengths but was inspired by Allah to attack his weakness. Prophet Joseph also used strategy very effectively. In *Surah Yusuf*, he planned a scenario that would shame his brothers into repentance. By placing a drinking cup in one of his brothers' saddlebag and accusing them of theft, he prompted them to admit their real crime and deal with their past misdeed. Finally, as pointed out by Altalib,[4] Prophet Noah reacted in a proactive strategic manner by building the ark before the flood, selecting pairs of animals, and working collaboratively with the believers.

This strategic awareness shown by the prophets is but a reflection of the planning of the Supreme Strategist, the One whose Message they were spreading. Repeatedly, the Qur'an reminds us that Allah is the best planner. For example, Allah talks about His planning (Qur'an, 86:15) or the signs of His Perfect Plan. For example, He refers to the careful crafting of the natural environment as one of His signs:

أَلَمْ تَرَ أَنَّ ٱللَّهَ أَنزَلَ مِنَ ٱلسَّمَاءِ مَاءً فَأَخْرَجْنَا بِهِۦ ثَمَرَٰتٍ مُّخْتَلِفًا أَلْوَٰنُهَا ۚ وَمِنَ ٱلْجِبَالِ جُدَدٌ بِيضٌ وَحُمْرٌ مُّخْتَلِفٌ أَلْوَٰنُهَا وَغَرَابِيبُ سُودٌ ۝ وَمِنَ ٱلنَّاسِ وَٱلدَّوَآبِّ وَٱلْأَنْعَٰمِ مُخْتَلِفٌ أَلْوَٰنُهُۥ كَذَٰلِكَ ۗ إِنَّمَا يَخْشَى ٱللَّهَ مِنْ عِبَادِهِ ٱلْعُلَمَٰٓؤُا۟ ۗ إِنَّ ٱللَّهَ عَزِيزٌ غَفُورٌ ۝

WHAT IS STRATEGIC MANAGEMENT?

> *Do you not see that Allah sends down rain from the sky? With it, We then bring out produce of various colors. In addition, in the mountains are tracts white and red, of various shades of color and black, intense in hue. And so among men and crawling creatures and cattle are they of various colors. Those truly fear Allah among His Servants who have knowledge: For Allah is exalted in Might, Oft-Forgiving.* (Qur'an, 35:27-28)

His Plan encompasses everything. No matter how perfectly one may plan, Allah is the Decider.

أَفَأَمِنُواْ مَكْرَ ٱللَّهِ ۚ فَلَا يَأْمَنُ مَكْرَ ٱللَّهِ إِلَّا ٱلْقَوْمُ ٱلْخَٰسِرُونَ ۝

> *Did they, then, feel secure against Allah's Plan? But no one can feel secure against the Plan of Allah except those (doomed) to ruin!* (Qur'an, 7:99)

> "There is no intelligence greater than planning."
> – Prophet Muhammad

Pharaoh's relentless pursuit of Moses and the Israelites, the self-serving plan of Joseph's brothers to kill him, and Zulaykha's cunning entrapment of Joseph are examples of how Allah's Plan defeated those of various individuals. The stories of 'Ad (Qur'an, *surah* 11) and Thamud (Qur'an, *surah* 7) also remind us of the plight of nations that were destroyed when they became arrogant and transgressed the limits that He had set for humanity.

The fact of Allah's plan should not deter us from planning, as long as we acknowledge His supremacy. In many circumstances, planning is helpful and may provide an advantage. This is why Prophet Muhammad said: "There is no intelligence greater than planning."[5] Many incidents in his life reflected strategic planning: the migrants from Makkah to Madinah in September 622 CE followed a route that was exactly the opposite of what his pursuers had anticipated. Inspired by Allah, he concluded the treaty of Hudaybiyyah, which turned out to be a clear victory for the Muslims and provided a much-needed strategic, short-term respite. Immediately after agreeing to this treaty, he preempted the Companions' apparent lethargy by following the advice of one of his wives, Umm Salamah, to slaughter his sacrificial animal first. Positioning the Muslims' army, draining the well at Badr, positioning the Muslim archers on Badr's hills, and using

1
WHAT IS STRATEGIC MANAGEMENT?

the trench as a defensive technique at Khandaq are vivid testimonies of the Prophet's appreciation of planning and stratagems.

Shar`i* and *Tabi` Principles of Strategic Planning

The Shari`ah clearly describes the efficient and effective conduct of Islamic for-profit and not-for-profit organizations as being encompassed within the concept of *ihsan* (excellence). When Islamic organizations seek to incorporate Islamic values in their *modus operandi*, they resort to the Shari`ah's guidelines. However, the Shari`ah does not enunciate operationally how an organization is to achieve sustainable competitive advantage in a highly turbulent, hypercompetitive environment. Rosly draws a distinction between *shar`i* and *tabi`* principles in business strategy.[6]

Overall, the strategic conduct of any Islamic business can be segmented into two areas: *shar`i* and *tabi`*. As Rosly indicates, "The Tabi` principles (i.e., the rational and empirical – an aspect of dunya [the world]) relate to the mundane where man applies reason and experience to run his daily business, while the *Shari`* principles (i.e., Allah's command) convey the Divine rules that man must observe [while] doing the same. Both shall remain inseparable. The rational and empirical are driven by the spiritual values of the Qur'an."[7]

Since the *shar`i* principles are derived from the Qur'an and the Sunnah, they are common in all aspects of business transactions: Islamic banking, treatment of employees, conduct of partnerships, and so on. These principles originating from Allah separate the *halal* (lawful) from the *haram* (forbidden) and are intended to foster justice (`adalah) in business transactions. When those engaged in business behave according to the Shari`ah's principles, they are fulfilling the *akhirah's* (Hereafter) requirements of the Islamic worldview.

While the Shari`ah's principles describe how Islamic transactions are to be conducted in a just and equitable manner, other dimensions of market activity need not depend on explicit divine guidance. This is the *tabi`* (natural) aspect of market activities that defines efficiency and, therefore, performance. It is nature's way. *Tabi`* values, which are universal, can be used by all people, irrespective of faith and belief. For example, a company can increase output by reducing per unit costs. In economics and in manufacturing, this process is known to achieve economies of scale. To increase sales, a business should first conduct market research. To manage a complex multi-billion dollar project, it

> *Tabi`* principles relate to the mundane where man applies reason and experience to run his daily business whereas *shar`i* principles convey the Divine rules that man must observe simultaneously.

should use such project management techniques as PERT (Program Evaluation Review Technique). The *tabi`* aspect of a business cannot be ignored, even when it runs under an Islamic label, for both Muslims and non-Muslims are expected to obey it. Its use is not so much about faith (*iman*) as it is about efficiency and competence – although ethics (*akhlaq*) always apply to Muslims' conduct.

Thus, when mapping out a strategy, one notices that the Shari`ah does not describe the strategic management process and its associated techniques, and that Shari`ah scholars are not trained to be strategy experts. They can only help business people keep the *halal* distinct from the *haram* based on Qur'anic injunctions. Consider the case of Islamic financial planning: After screening for *halal* and *haram* investment instruments and areas, the *tabi`* aspects become dominant process criteria in terms of the price-earnings ratio, return on investment, earnings per share, and other financial performance measures.

Similarly, as an Islamic organization seeks to develop and implement its strategy using *tabi`* principles, it must always make sure that it observes *shar`i* principles. As Rosly stresses,[8] knowledge derived from non-divine sources (i.e., human) cannot be downgraded as ungodly, for the `*aql* (reason) is also divine in nature. Humanity can discover Allah by thinking about and contemplating His Signs. The `*aql* is a powerful instrument to explain the nature and, therefore, the greatness of Allah. However, if it is deprived of divine guidance, it becomes short-sighted and unable to produce credible *tabi`* principles for humanity's enjoyment.

Key Concepts in Strategic Management

Strategic management deals with the organization's behavior within its external market, and its internal roles, processes, structure, and decisions in order to enable the organization to function at its peak within that external environment.[9] Strategic management asks three basic questions: Where are we going? Where could we be going? How do we get there?[10]

Strategic management involves both strategy formulation and strategy implementation. The two primary phases of strategy formulation are commonly referred to as strategic planning and tactical or operational planning. Formulating either a strategic or an operational plan is relatively easy, given that anyone can sit down and come up with a wonderful list of resolutions or goals. But implementing a plan is much

> Strategic management asks three basic quetions: Where are we going? Where could we be going? How do we get there?

1
WHAT IS STRATEGIC MANAGEMENT?

more challenging, and this is where the most effective organizations – whether Muslim or not – engage in strategy-supportive action.

In contrast, a typical Islamic organization rarely transitions to implementation.[11] It often forgets that strategic thinking needs to be built into everything it does. In each of its actions and activities, you and your organization need to be strategically aware and ask how this action or activity relates to your overall strategy and how it brings you closer to our ultimate aim: serving the Creator.

Strategic planning can be defined as "the process by which the guiding members of an organization envision its future and develop the necessary procedures and operations to achieve that future."[12] Bryson regards it as "a disciplined effort to produce fundamental decisions and actions that shape and guide what an organization is, what it does, and why it does it."[13] When these definitions are taken together, we notice certain key elements. Strategic planning:

- Encompasses decisions and actions that have a long-term impact,
- Is a process that enables decision makers to be proactive,
- Involves identifying the organization's idealized potential and working toward it, and
- Provides a framework that allows for internal consistency among all of the decisions and activities of the organization's various sections.

An operational plan builds upon the strategic plan emerging from the strategic planning process and focuses on specific short-term actions and results. After developing a strategic and an operational plan, you implement your strategy by acting upon it. Remember that there is no such thing as a perfect strategic plan; an organization that spends too much time perfecting a plan is spending too little time implementing it. This endless fine-tuning instead of acting is referred to as "analysis-paralysis." How many communities have spent months or years planning the perfect mosque location or perfecting their Islamic school curriculum, only to find out that they have lost a whole generation of Muslim youths who could wait no longer? As General Patton once said, "A good plan executed today is better than a perfect plan implemented next week."[14]

> Strategic planning is the process by which organization decision-makers determine where the organization is heading, what its self-concept is, what its long-term priorities are and how it will achieve them.

Why Strategic Management?

Strategic management is important because, if properly planned, executed, and monitored, it facilitates the move toward excellence in the running of an organization. In particular, strategic management:

- Enhances the organization's ability to be proactive, anticipate problems, and stay focused on both the future and the present.
- Allows decisions to be based on the best alternatives, since they stem from the group's consensus (*shura*). Therefore, it encourages the best possible judgment based on what is frequently very little information.
- Improves the participants' understanding and motivations, since they are following a clear and consistent vision.
- Instills unity and internal consistency among all decisions and actions.
- Provides a cognitive frame of reference to guide decision makers, even if the situation on the ground makes the plan obsolete.
- Facilitates strategy implementation and decreases resistance to change. This advantage is similar to what is derived from the consultative dimension of Theory Z (Japanese management). Japanese managers discovered that when they involve personnel in the decisions that affect them and include their insights and suggestions, implementation is smoother and faster. Similarly, involving personnel during the strategy formulation stage facilitates strategy implementation.
- Helps to channel resources to the critical areas, according to your strategic plan's long-term priorities, and to areas where you will see the most effective results.
- Incorporates strategic thinking into your organization's way of doing things, and provides a template for determining which aspects of the external environment matter the most.
- Integrates a proactive and disciplined stance into the organization, and
- Takes into account the long-term consequences of current decisions.

In our quest to serve Allah, one of strategic management's most important goals is to attain excellence. Shaddad ibn Aws relates, in *Sahih*

> The concept of *ihsan* demands that Muslims achieve excellence in every *halal* endeavor they engage in.

1
WHAT IS STRATEGIC MANAGEMENT?

Muslim (hadith no. 4810), that Prophet Muhammad taught: "God has ordained excellence in everything [...]."[15] In this regard, the Qur'an emphasizes that one's reward should be commensurate with one's effort (Qur'an 3:136, 99:7, and 48:19). This rule applies to the immediate reward in this life as well as the deferred reward in the Hereafter. One's work is rewarded not only by other people, but also by Allah (Qur'an, 50:30).

This idea of *ihsan* correlates with the concept of a sustainable competitive advantage (SCA). In the corporate world, achieving SCA means that a firm occupies an industry position that leads to superior performance over 10 or more years.[16] SCA is not easy to achieve. Many Islamic institutions have short bursts of excellent performance, but then dwindle to mediocrity and barely linger on before vanishing. SCA is achieved by outliers, those few that take time to be strategically aware and pursue excellence in a determined and relentless manner. Two excellent examples of such organizations are the Council of American Islamic Relations (CAIR: www.cair-net.org) and Indian Muslim Relief and Charities (IMRC: www.imrc.ws). When the performance of Islamic institutions is examined over several years, it tends to regress toward the mean. According to Hawawini, Subramanian, and Verdin,[17] only a small minority of firms achieves a sustainable competitive advantage. Amazingly, these excellent companies are rarely the ones seeking the public limelight, and their leaders try to avoid being put on a pedestal.[18] Similarly, although the Islamic Society of North America (ISNA: www.isna.net) and the Muslim Students' Association of the USA and Canada (MSA: www.msanational.org) have in the past achieved great success by the Grace of Allah, the organizations that have recently excelled in North America are relatively small and new: CAIR and IMRC.

Explanations for the inability of once-leading Islamic organizations and businesses to achieve excellence or SCA are many and obvious. These reasons include:

- A lack of attention to and understanding of strategic management,
- An overly narrow understanding and application of the Qur'an and the Prophet's *sirah* (e.g., should Muslims living in a non-Muslim country become involved in politics and other issues?)
- Structural and cultural inertia,
- Structure of the niche or domain (being more monopolistic or oligopolistic),

> One of the major drawbacks of Islamic organizations is an emphasis on the good old boy's network, or on *'asabiyyah*.

- Leadership succession with an emphasis on dynasty, a good old boys' network, or `asabiyyah (parochial loyalty to one's group, clan, or tribe),
- Poor use of inadequate resources,
- Living in the past and focusing solely on past achievements,
- Inability to adapt to a changing environment, and to respond to, the changing needs of both Muslims and people from other faith-based communities,
- An apathetic and aging membership, and
- Obsolete competencies, including a distrust of modern technology.

Unfortunately, these reasons tend to apply to many Islamic and non-Islamic organizations throughout the world.

To reverse their organizational sclerosis, Islamic leaders must master strategic management so that they can enhance their ability to engage in "down-board," as opposed to immediate, thinking.[19] For example, world-class soccer players not only think about their immediate moves, but also look "down board" by anticipating their opponents' likely responses to their moves and thus think several moves ahead. Strategic planning is quite similar: Planners must look down-board, assess the implications of their plans, and then formulate additional plans based on those contingencies. An excellent example of this took place in 4 AH, when the Prophet sought the Banu Nadir tribe's help.[20] While among them, he found out that they were planning to kill him right then and there. Knowing that he had to take decisive action, the Prophet left their settlement on the outskirts of Madinah, returned to the city's center, summoned Muhammad ibn Maslamah, and told him to inform the Banu Nadir that they had to leave Madinah within ten days because of their treacherous behavior. This proactive strategic stance preempted major future problems.

The Prophet engaged in "down board" thinking.

The Strategic Management Model

Our model of strategic management integrates across a number of models currently available, but also stresses Islamic values and beliefs at its core. This model (figure 1) is oriented toward Islamic organizations, whether for-profit or nonprofit. Unlike other models, it covers both strategy formulation and implementation, as well as performance assessment, and emphasizes ethics monitoring and adjustment. For a non-profit Islamic organization or a Muslim business, this emphasis

1
WHAT IS STRATEGIC MANAGEMENT?

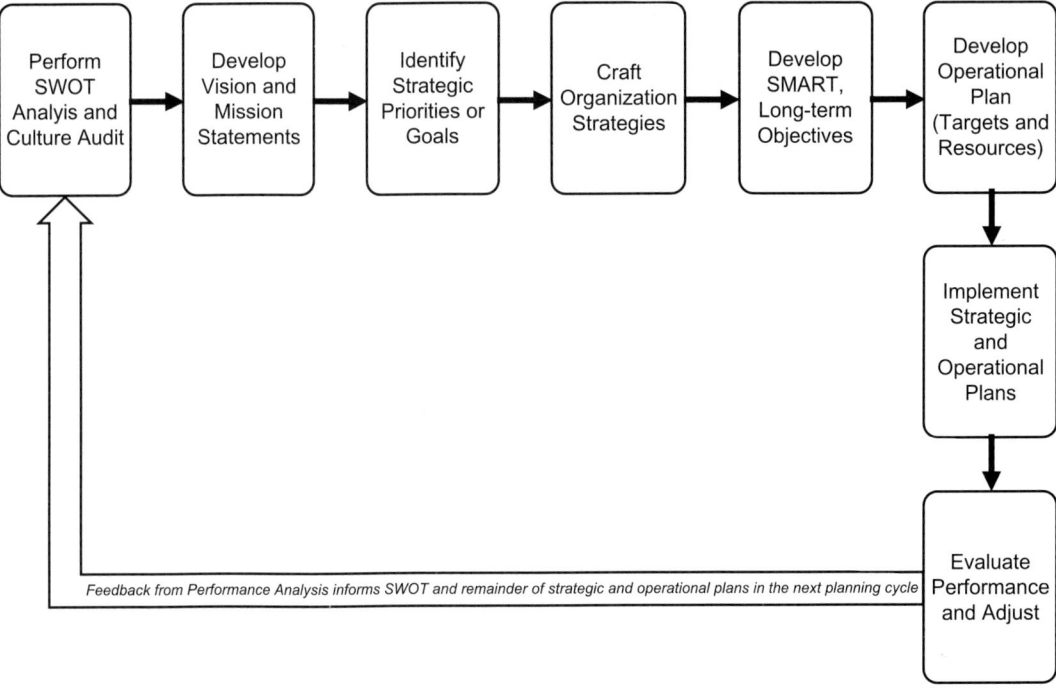

Figure 1
The Strategic Management Process for an Islamic Organization

permeates the entire strategic management process, for work is considered part of a Muslim's `ibadah (worship).

The eight tasks of strategic management include the strategy formulation phase (viz., conducting a SWOT analysis, developing a vision and a mission, listing one's goals or strategic priorities, developing long-term objectives and strategies, formulating shorter-term objectives or targets, and assessing resource needs) and the strategy implementation phase (viz., matching the organization structure, culture, and leadership to the strategic and operational plans, and, finally, evaluation and adjustment).

Typically, these eight tasks are sequential. However, they can be revisited if they need to be re-calibrated. Hence, the strategic management process is an evolutionary, not a linear, process that never stops. The end product of the strategic planning phase is an integrative yet flexible plan. This, then, is where the strategy implementation phase starts.

> The strategic management process is an evolutionary and dynamic process that never stops once it is initiated.

Each task listed in the strategic management model will be analyzed in its own chapter. Now, I present a glossary[21] of key strategic management terms:

Glossary of Key Strategy Terms	
Vision Statement	An idealized expression of what the organization seeks to become in the future; a view of an organization's future direction.
Mission Statement	A statement reflecting what the organization seeks to do for a specific group of customers, and how distinctive its contribution will be.
Goals	The strategic issues/priority areas where the organization intends to focus its attention and resources. Goals need to be clearly linked to the mission statement.
Strategies	Strategies explain how we are going to get from where we are now to where we envision ourselves to be in the future. Strategies are crafted at different managerial levels: organizational or corporate level strategies, divisional (strategic business units) strategies, functional strategies, and operating strategies. Each level of strategy has different concerns.
Objectives	Objectives are tied to specific goals and represent a managerial commitment to producing specified results in a specified time frame. They spell out how much of what kind of performance by when. There may be multiple objectives for each goal.
Performance Measure	A measurement of efficiency, economy, or effectiveness linked to a specific objective.
Input	Labor hours, resources, equipment, or supplies – in short, whatever it takes to produce of a product or service.
Output	Units of products (including services) of an activity.
Outcome	The resulting effect (impact) of an output's use/application.

WHAT IS STRATEGIC MANAGEMENT?

Efficiency	Maximum output for a fixed input, or minimum input for a fixed output. Efficiency is always a ratio indicator.
Economy	Quantity of outputs or inputs of a certain quality level obtained at the minimum cost. Economy is a subset of efficiency.
Effectiveness	The delivery of a quality product or service that meets the needs of its intended customers or stakeholders.
Stakeholder	Organizations, groups, or individuals (both internal and external) with an interest in the operation and/or success of the organization (or division or functional area) delivering a product or service.
Customer	Organizations, groups, or individuals using the products or services of an organization (division or functional area). Customers can be either internal or external.

Pitfalls of Strategic Management

Strategic management, like any other management technique, does not guarantee success and thus needs to be implemented wisely. The SPC (strategic planning committee) or the organization's leadership can easily fall victim to the following pitfalls if they are not cautious:

- Splitting planning from other management tasks (the fallacy of detachment). Many Muslim organizations involved in strategic planning think that planners are separate or sometimes even "better" than implementers. When this takes place, planners can easily dream up unachievable plans that others will have to implement. Another example is when planners feel that they know "best" about everything because they have been there the "longest" or have contributed the most financially since the organization was established.

- Overemphasizing a myopic, number-crunching approach (the fallacy of formalization). As Grant points out, the systematization arising from formal procedures hampers flexibility and organizational learning.[22] Islamic organizations often use an overly complex, quantitative approach to strategic planning. Numbers can serve as a guide, but they cannot be the sole basis of deciding an organization's long-term direction.

WHAT IS STRATEGIC MANAGEMENT?

- Demanding unattainable results from subordinates or followers. When decision-makers set up goals that are too optimistic or that require resources that implementers lack or have no control over, it is likely that these results are simply unrealistic. Demanding that results be achieved no matter what can lead to discouragement, rebellion, or even learned helplessness. An Islamic Sunday school is unlikely to succeed if it has only one teacher, 75 students (of varying ages and levels of preparation), and no support staff.

- Being unable to adapt to rapidly changing environments. Leaders of Islamic organizations often assume that their strategic plan is immutable, and so are reluctant to adjust it. This absolutist approach to strategic management is a serious miscalculation, because external stakeholders will often counter the organization's strategic plan. Unless some flexibility is built into the plan, very little will be accomplished. Internal stakeholders may also resist change and engage in delaying tactics, such as stonewalling changes until the overly vocal or active leader or board member can be voted out of office. Several decades ago, the U.S. State Department fell victim to this problem when career diplomats simply waited out the political appointee who was their temporary boss and did not implement any of his changes.

- Drowning in data. One can get so enamored with data gathering that he or she may forget that the emphasis is on getting work done in an organized framework as outlined by a strategic plan. As a result, one Islamic organization that I know of gathered so much data that it rarely had enough time to distill it into any usable information. Moreover, its leaders did not have the statistical expertise to analyze the data adequately.

- The fallacy of prediction. The external environment cannot be predicted. In Islam, only Allah knows the future with certainty, and "prediction" is, at best, an inexact art. Quite a few organizations believe that they have more insight into the course of future events than they actually have. As a result, they are often surprised when only very little of what they "predicted" actually happens. As Muslims, we do what the Prophet suggested: Tie our camel and trust in Allah. Strategic planning is simply tying our camel, and the rest is *tawakkul* (putting our trust in Allah).[23] I will discuss this concept of *tawakkul* in a later chapter.

> Strategic planning is simply 'tying our camel', and putting our trust in Allah (*tawakkul*).

CHAPTER 2

PRE-PLANNING

If you are initiating the strategic planning process in an Islamic organization, first determine whether the organization is ready. Be sure not to gloss over the preparations during the pre-planning stage.

Readiness for strategic planning is difficult to ascertain. Generally, it means that the organization's key stakeholders (e.g., the board of directors, the leader, the major donors or investors, or the primary organizational participants) have decided to commit the necessary time and resources to engage in the strategic management process, that everyone supports the process, that the resulting decisions will be respected and not sabotaged, and that the most competent and appropriate people will be empowered to see the plan through. Meritocracy, rather than 'asabiyyah or even nepotism based on family or friendship, will be emphasized. This is consistent with the Prophet's following hadith:

> *Whoever delegates a position to someone whereas he sees someone else as more competent (for the position), verily he has cheated Allah and His Apostle and all the Muslims.*[1]

This hadith refers to the most competent person, without selectively attributing competence to men. Some Islamic organizations consistently overlook, downplay, or even ignore our sisters' contributions, forgetting that Khadija was a very successful businesswoman before

> A stakeholder is anyone or any party who has a claim or interest in what the organization does.

PRE-PLANNING

she married the Prophet and that Aisha made an everlasting contribution to numerous hadiths. Sisters like Aisha Lemu in Nigeria or Amina Assilmi in North America have made positive contributions to the Islamic landscape in their own countries and worldwide.

Setting up an appropriate Strategic Planning Committee (SPC) is critical to effective strategic planning and implementation.

Once your organization demonstrates its readiness for the strategic management process, you and the other decision makers need to decide who will be involved, what are the planning and implementation timelines, how to evaluate performance based on the plan, and what financial or other resources will be needed. The Strategic Planning Committee (SPC) members will contribute both to the strategic planning process' quality as well as to the quality of the plan's final version. If some resources are unavailable, the SPC members will have to consider how and by whom the available resources will be procured, and when they will be made available.

Overall, you must assess *a priori* if the organization is truly committed to the strategic management process. If the requisite willingness is present, use the *shura* process to appoint the SPC's members. Then, educate them about the strategic management process.

Commitment Toward the Strategic Management Process

Any major organizational change requires the commitment of the organization's leadership. Adopting the strategic management process is one of the most demanding and intrusive changes that any organization can make. Unless top-level commitment is present, all strategies or macro-level change programs adopted will be unsuccessful.[2]

Islamic organizations in the West have very diverse members originating from countries or areas with diverse cultural values and norms.

Key variables that affect an organization's commitment to change are previous experience with organizational change attempts, the leadership's attitude to change (proactive vs. reactive), and tolerance for change within the organizational and national culture. Some organizations have a fluid internal environment, due to the introduction of multiple change programs, and therefore are less afraid of strategic change. Others that are more bureaucratic and quite set in their ways view any type of change as a threat. People who attend the mosque or who work in a business are often from different generations and hold a different set of priorities. They may have difficulty communicating peaceably. Some countries have a culture that is less tolerant of change or high in uncertainty avoidance,[3] while others may have a culture that is high in power distance (i.e., blind obedience to their superiors). Thus, when such diverse groups come together in a common setting, such as an Islamic center or a global organization like

IIFSO (the International Islamic Federation of Student Organizations), leaders must devise strategies that will transcend these cultural differences.

Independent of their previous experience with change attempts and their organization's tolerance for change, an organization's leaders must be in the forefront of the strategic management process. They must be absolutely committed to this new path and not view it as a fad.

Forming the SPC (Strategic Planning Committee)

In general, the SPC should have from 7 to 12 members. The larger the group, the less any single team member will be able to participate and the greater the likelihood of fragmentation and/or polarization. The existence of opposing factions causes the decision-making process to suffer. In addition, larger groups make it extremely difficult to schedule joint meetings.

Even with a committee composed of 7 to 12 people, the SPC's membership should be diverse in background and expertise in order to avoid *groupthink*.[4] Members of a group experiencing groupthink exhibit a drive toward consensus that is usually achieved at any cost while dissent is suppressed. A vivid example of this dysfunctional group process took place during President Kennedy's planning to invade Cuba. The planning group was so self-confident and so mesmerized by Kennedy's charismatic personality that no one challenged him. As a result, the planners never looked at a map of Cuba. The results of this groupthink led to the Bay of Pigs fiasco, where the Cuban military intercepted the American invading forces and left them no viable escape route. To avoid this poor group practice, participants from diverse backgrounds and representing multiple key stakeholder segments should be pulled together to offer a variety of perspectives.

A useful technique for putting together an SPC is to conduct a *stakeholder analysis*.[5] A stakeholder is any person or group who is (or is likely) to be significantly affected by your organization's actions. Identifying those people and involving *a priori* those who will implement your strategic plan will enable you to build a common, shared frame of reference and encourage everyone on the team to pull together and work toward a unified direction. However, stakeholders are not to be weighed equally; they are either *primary* or *secondary*. Primary stakeholders are those with whom you interact directly, such as your customers. Secondary stakeholders are those who are on your organization's periphery and come in direct contact with

Groupthink takes place when members of a group push for consensus while suppressing any type of dissent.

you only intermittently (e.g., the public-at-large). Stakeholders can transform themselves from primary to secondary and vice-versa, depending upon the situation.

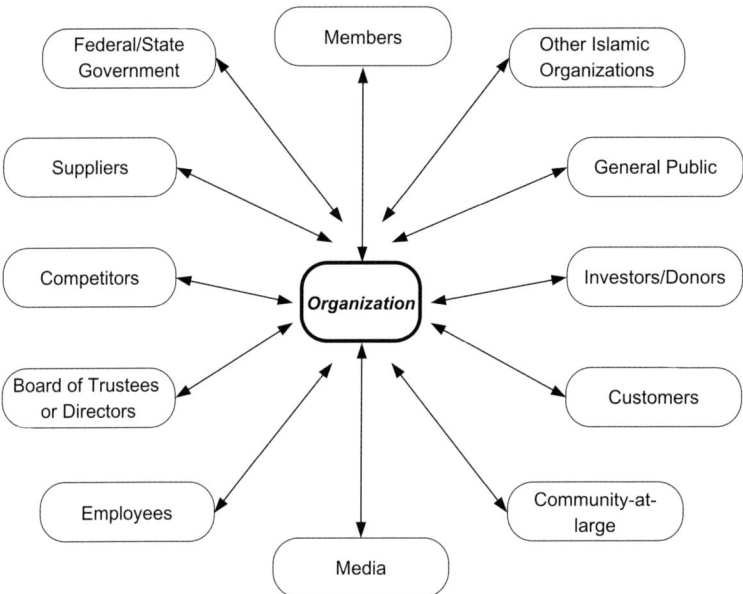

Figure 2
Stakeholder Map

To make sure that no relevant stakeholders are left out or ignored, consider using a stakeholder map (figure 2). When selecting SPC members, the following questions may be useful:
- What is his/her attitude toward the change process?
- What value does he/she add to the strategic plan's overall quality? Usually, a primary stakeholder such as your customer can be expected to provide high value-added input. Although competitors are primary stakeholders too, you probably would not want to include them on your SPC.
- Is his/her commitment necessary for successful implementation?
- What is his/her team spirit?

You may have noticed that none of the above questions focus on the potential SPC member's level of Islamic behavior. This is because the SPC is a competence-based group. While it is desirable to have stakeholders who are practicing Muslims, they need not be flawless, as long as they are sincere and making an effort. Worksheet #1 (Appendix A, p. 164) has been designed to help you select SPC members.

Preparing the SPC and the Organization

Organization members resist change not because they oppose the change itself, but because of the uncertainties associated with it.[6] The introduction of strategic planning and implementation is a macro-level, organizational change that is likely to create a lot of uncertainty and intra-organizational stress. To preempt any internal and external resistance to change, communicate the whole process and possible changes as transparently and as understandably as possible to the relevant stakeholders.

> Organization members resist change not necessarily because they oppose the change itself, but rather because of the uncertainties associated with it.

Once you have selected the SPC, announce the news to your members or stockholders. This type of communication will allow you to obtain their buy-in as well as provide you with the opportunity to seek their assistance and feedback during this process. You may do any or all of the following:

- Announce the news in the presence of the board of trustees (or board of directors) and the SPC chair, or with the president or CEO present. The latter should already be privy to the information about to be disclosed; do not spring the news as a "surprise."
- Explain the rationale for strategic planning, the tangible outputs and benefits to be derived, and how the members/stockholders can provide their input. If this process has been attempted before, explain why you are initiating it again and why it will be different this time around. Stress your personal commitment to the strategic management process.
- Announce the process in the organization's official newsletter (to the larger public) and with a memo to request everybody's cooperation (including the staff).
- List the SPC's members and explain why they were selected. Provide the name of an SPC member who can serve as a liaison between the committee and the rest of the organization.
- Be clear about the projected time frames for the strategic and operational plans, as well as their implementation.
- Ask for and answer any feedback or concerns.

PRE-PLANNING

Make a copy of this or a similar book available to all SPC members, and place at least one copy in the mosque library for the general membership to peruse. Keeping all of the organization's members well-informed about the strategic planning process and the progress and direction of the planning team is essential.

Most importantly, you, as the leader, cannot simply initiate the process and then leave the SPC on its own. Unless you are deeply committed and hold key people responsible for the plan's subsequent implementation, the other members will not take the planning process seriously. In an Islamic organization that I once worked with, the leader delegated the initiation and implementation to a board member and then stepped back. In spite of my best efforts to get him involved more directly, he did not wish to take a more hands-on approach. The SPC's members, the remainder of the board, and the lower echelons in the hierarchy promptly understood that he was uncomfortable with the process. As a result, implementation has been slow and laborious.

The Pledge

Prior to developing and implementing a strategic plan, it is imperative that the leader and his/her SPC, as well as the key decision-makers and stakeholders, pledge to do the following:

1. Publicly commit themselves to the process. Announce their intention at the annual general assembly or meeting of members, repeat it in the organization's newsletter/magazine, post it on highly visible notice boards, and describe it on the organization's website;
2. Take responsibility for championing and implementing the plan;
3. Provide tangible support to those who effectively implement their part of the plan. Even when the implementation suffers setbacks, the leader should encourage those who are doing their best to help move the strategic plan forward. In the battle of Mu'tah, Khalid ibn Walid withdrew the Muslim forces from the battlefield and returned to Madinah because he realized that his army was outnumbered. When they reached Madinah, the Muslims cried out: "O you who have fled! You have fled from the way of Allah." The Prophet restrained them, saying:

> Since implementing a strategic plan is hard work, leaders should encourage their followers even when they fail, and stress that failures represent learning opportunities—like Khalid ibn Walid did at Mut'ah.

20   Strategic Planning and Implementation for Islamic Organizations

"They have not fled. They shall return to fight, if Allah wills it."[7] This encouragement proved decisive, for Muslims never lost a battle whenever Khalid led their army.

Time Commitment

The SPC and the organization's leadership must set aside adequate time for the strategic planning process' initial and subsequent annual cycles. Drafting your first strategic plan can usually be done during an off-site retreat and may last anywhere from 2 to 7 days. Worksheet #2 (Appendix A, p. 165) is designed to help you organize the planning binder for your SPC's first strategic planning retreat. Initially, the strategic planning process (involving the full-fledged development of both a strategic and an operational plan) may take about 2 to 3 months, with the SPC spending a total of about 50-200 hours. The length of time required to develop both the strategic and the operational plans depends on the organization's size, the scope and complexity of its products or services, and its previous experience with the strategic management process.

In between the SPC's meetings, the staff will be on hand to compile the data that the committee needs. In later years, a strategic planning retreat of about 2.5-5 days should be adequate to review and adjust the strategic plan. Typically, the retreat should coincide with the beginning of the new budgeting cycle.

During the initial or yearly strategic planning retreat, the SPC may meet anywhere, as long as it is not at the organization's site and/or during work hours. Off-site meetings are preferred so that interruptions and other disruptions from the work environment can be prevented. Whether this is the first time a plan is being initiated or whether the organization is experienced in the planning process and doing its annual plan cycle, there may be a reasonable gap of 1 week to about 1 month between developing the strategic plan and outlining the operational plan in detail. This is because the people developing the strategic plan may not be the ones developing the operational plan, and thus may not have the fine-grained information necessary to flesh out the day-to-day operational details. The length of the time gap between these two undertakings is a function of the organization's size and the scope and complexity of what it does.

> An off-site strategic planning retreat is a more inspiring venue for developing or reviewing your organization's strategic plan.

PRE-PLANNING

The Role of the Board of Directors

Since the primary responsibility for formulating and implementing a strategic plan falls on you, as the leader, together with the help of the SPC and your key managers/committee chairs, your organization's board of directors (usually called the *majlis al-shura*) must supervise the change process implied by the strategic plan and ensure that the strategic management process fulfills the overall intent of the relevant primary stakeholders. The fallout from 9/11 in America and the July 7 bombings in the United Kingdom, the Patriot Act or its tentacular variants in other countries, the potential of lawsuits against the board of directors itself and the need for indemnification insurance require careful clarification of the board's responsibilities, whether they are not-for-profit or for-profit.

Often, however, board members of leading Islamic organizations or mosques find it hard to meet the challenges associated with their role. A major reason for this is because they are habitually chosen or elected on the basis of their previous contribution to the organization rather than their ability to meet its future needs.[8] Some mosques require that potential board members make exceedingly large monetary donations to be eligible – long after the mosque's capital projects have been completed. Other mosques select board members based on their ability to give a *khutbah* (Friday sermon) – even after an imam has been hired. In a worst-case scenario, some board members are chosen based on clan, family, or nationality criteria.

Irrespective of how your board members were selected, you are likely to submit the strategic plan to them for their review and approval before initiating the implementation stage. Unfortunately, boards often operate under rigid constraints. Sometimes, outside directors do not have the deep inside knowledge necessary to propose any strategy alternatives in lieu of those embedded in the strategic plan under review. At other times, the board is viewed as a rubber-stamp entity whose only purpose is to confer an aura of legitimacy to the decisions already taken by the organization's president, CEO, or executive director. A board that serves at the top decision maker's whim rarely controls its own agenda and is almost never consulted during the strategy formulation phase

How can an Islamic organization's board of directors fulfill its oversight role more effectively? An in-depth study of boards of directors pro-

PRE-PLANNING

> Leaders and boards of directors must not use a hands-off approach after the strategic plan is developed. What is not measured and inspected will not be accomplished.

vides some key clues.[9] First, this board of directors needs comparative data on the organization over a specific time period (e.g., this year as compared to the previous five years) and comparative information on current and future competitors. This data must not be gathered haphazardly, but must instead relate to a small, but information-rich set of performance indicators (to be covered in chapter 14).

Second, the board of directors needs the time and opportunity to study the organization's strategy and be able to provide meaningful input. In that regard, board meetings crammed into one day and running over 8 hours are rarely useful. Further, quite a few Islamic organizations either gather a lot of irrelevant data that is not converted to useful information or are reluctant to provide any data to their board of directors. In fact, some executive directors I have encountered were quite defensive when asked to provide comparative data, and their organization's president was reluctant to press for more information.

Third, the board of directors needs counter-power – the ability to "counterbalance top management."[10] They must have a chairman who is not the president. In addition, they must be able to control the meeting agenda and evaluate the president, the vice-presidents, and the division heads, as well as the executive directors, on an annual basis. Boards that have this type of counter-power and that have more outsiders, rather than insiders, tend to be more effective than boards that have no counter-power and that are dominated by insiders. Boards with little power tend to metamorphose into caretakers and are less likely to be proactive and participative.[11]

Finally, from an Islamic viewpoint, board members must be selected on the basis of their competence (see the hadith cited on page 15). Such competencies may require interacting with the political system, excelling at interfaith activities, acting as a spokesperson to a disparate set of external actors, including the media, and so on.

When monitoring the strategic management process from afar, a properly chosen and empowered board of directors does not have to challenge everything being proposed or undertaken – especially if the organization is on track. Should the organization be experiencing difficulty, its directors must be more forthright and firm in order to rectify the situation. Bitter medicine may have to be administered as the board or an external independent audit group commissioned by the board submits your organization's executive leadership to rigorous scrutiny.

CHAPTER 3

SWOT ANALYSIS

SWOT involves assessing the internal strengths and weaknesses and the external opportunities and threats.

As shown in figure 1, the first task in the strategic management process is conducting a SWOT analysis. SWOT is an acronym for Strengths (S), Weaknesses (W), Opportunities (O), and Threats (T). An organization's SPC and stakeholders, including its leaders and followers, must always track its internal strengths and weaknesses, as well as its external opportunities and threats. Decision-makers need to understand and assess both what is happening within the organization and in the external environment.

Environmental Scanning

No organization exists in a vacuum, and ignoring its external environment will not safeguard it from external forces. The Prophet was intensely aware of the need to gather intelligence about, and keep track of, the external environment. This aspect of strategic leadership is discussed in *Leadership: An Islamic Perspective*.[1] Given below is an example from the Prophet's *sirah* of how Hudhayfah ibn al-Yaman kept him informed of external environmental threats during the danger-prone period of early Islam:

> Hudhayfah (ibn al-Yaman) had three qualities which particularly impressed the Prophet: his unique intelligence which he employed in dealing with difficult situations; his

SWOT ANALYSIS

quick wittedness and spontaneous response to the call for action, and his ability to keep a secret even under persistent questioning.

A noticeable policy of the Prophet was to bring out and use the special qualities and strengths of each individual companion of his. In deploying his companions, he was careful to choose the right man for the right task. This he did to excellent advantage in the case of Hudhayfah. One of the gravest problems the Muslims of Medina had to face was the existence in their midst of hypocrites (munafiqun) [...]. Although many of them had declared their acceptance of Islam, the change was only superficial and they continued to plot and intrigue against the Prophet and the Muslims.

Because of Hudhayfah's ability to keep a secret, the Prophet, peace be on him, confided in him the names of the munafiqun (hypocrites). It was a weighty secret which the Prophet did not disclose to any other of his companions. He gave Hudhayfah the task of watching the movements of the munafiqun, following their activities, and shielding the Muslims from the sinister danger they represented. It was a tremendous responsibility. The munafiqun, because they acted in secrecy and because they knew all the developments and plans of the Muslims from within, presented a greater threat to the community than the outright hostility of the kuffar.

From this time onwards, Hudhayfah was called "The Keeper of the Secret of the Messenger of Allah." Throughout his life, he remained faithful to his pledge not to disclose the names of the hypocrites. After the death of the Prophet, the Khalifah often came to him to seek his advice concerning their movements and activities, but he remained tight-lipped and cautious.[2]

Although figure 1 suggests that a SWOT analysis is done only initially, this really should be an ongoing activity. An organization has to monitor its internal and external environments continuously to determine where the organization's boundaries end and where the external environment begins, because it is often hard to distinguish between outsiders and

SWOT ANALYSIS

insiders. Members of the board of directors are often appointed from the outside and may not necessarily be considered insiders. As a result, decisions about what data to gather and who should receive it need to be made. An organization would not inadvertently want to give proprietary information to its competitors.

In carrying out a SWOT, Islamic organizations need to focus on value maximization: matching their best strengths to the most promising and attainable opportunities open to them.[3] Value maximization also means providing the best value-added service or product to your key stakeholder. If you are a business, your key stakeholder is your customer, not your stockholder. If you are an Islamic center, your key stakeholders are, typically, your near-by Muslim community, the Muslim community at large, and the other faith-based communities. Value-maximization requires a critical but difficult fit between the organization's internal configuration and the external environment, for this fit is dynamic and needs to be maintained in the midst of a turbulent environment.

> Value maximization also means providing the best value-added service or product to your key stakeholder or customer.

Internal Audit

The first part of a SWOT analysis is an audit of the organization's internal strengths and weaknesses and an assessment of its current state. An internal audit tells you what your organization can do by detailing its strengths and weaknesses. It enables you, as the leader, to uncover areas in which you might be able to develop a competitive advantage.

A strength is something that the organization excels at or a feature that makes it competitive, such as the following[4]:

- Human resources (e.g., experienced and motivated workers, managerial expertise, and deep leadership ranks).
- Competence or knowledge in a certain area (e.g., advocacy skills, web-based expertise, manufacturing prowess, or conference organizing).
- Ownership or control of key physical assets (e.g., location of facilities, first-mover advantage into certain geographical areas, and leading-edge technology).
- Financial resources (e.g., the equity in your company and actual cash – not pledged – donations).
- Intangible assets (e.g., customer goodwill, the organization's reputation and culture).
- Collaborative organizational relationships (e.g., inter-organizational

> Organizational strengths can be both tangible (e.g. physical assets) as well intangible (e.g. competence and good morale).

Strategic Planning and Implementation for Islamic Organizations   27

3
SWOT ANALYSIS

alliances). One example is the National Shura Council of North America, which brought together North America's four leading Islamic organizations for joint projects. A more recent example is the American Muslim Taskforce for Disaster Relief, which combines the efforts of 10 or more leading Islamic organizations in North America to help Muslims and non-Muslims whenever a natural disaster occurs. It is important to note here that your organization can engage in collaborative and competitive relationships with the same external entities simultaneously. For example, ISNA cooperates with ICNA (the Islamic Circle of North America) on such joint projects as the Bosnia Task Force, but competes with ICNA when fundraising or trying to serve the community.

While one could list innumerable organizational strengths, the strategic management literature indicates that organizations that outperform their rivals — independent of industry type — have *distinctive core competencies* that are sustainable over time.[5] Prahalad and Hamel define core competencies as "the collective learning in the organization, especially how to coordinate diverse production skills and integrate multiple streams of technologies."[6] Organizations must identify what competencies to focus on and then abandon those activities at which they are relatively weak and ineffective, and that do not advance their vision and mission. One key issue in this process is the ability to distinguish previous competencies from those that are about to come on-line or from prospective, future ones. For example, one leading Islamic organization held on to its manual processing membership function for too long, and thereby lost considerable momentum in its work.

While identifying your organization's strengths, make sure that you do not fall victim to the "curse of competence."[7] Indeed, it is very easy for an organization to be so successful using a specific core competency that its workers either do not develop other competencies or let them atrophy. Blinded by their own brilliance in one area, they miss very attractive new opportunities. An excellent example of this is IBM, the leading mainframe computer manufacturer in the world until 1979: The introduction of the personal computer took its leaders completely by surprise. They had totally overlooked the possibility that regular people might want a computer on their desk! Similarly, quite a few Islamic organizations are so good in one area (e.g., organizing conventions and conferences) that they miss other opportunities (e.g., building good relations

> The 'curse of competence' takes place either when an organization relies too much on a specific core competency at the expense of its other competencies or when it fails to develop future critical competencies.

with other faith-based communities). The curse of competence can also lead to arrogance, as some organizations overestimate their leaders' capabilities and underestimate Allah's contribution to their success. Given that Islamic history is replete with the ultimate demise of such arrogance, never overlook the potential liability of overestimating your organization's strengths or competencies.

> VRIO analysis provides a relatively balanced way of assessing your organization's strengths without falling victim to overconfidence.

A relatively balanced way of assessing your organization's strengths without falling prey to overconfidence is to use a VRIO (value, rarity, imitability, and organization) analysis. Barney and Hesterly suggest that you ask four questions when analyzing your strengths[8]:

1. **The Question of Value**: Does a strength enable your organization to take advantage of an external opportunity or counter an external threat? If not, this strength can potentially hamper your organization. Perhaps it is even a weakness. For example, your Islamic organization could claim leadership of the nation's Muslim community, but be unable to put together a national drive on a specific issue of concern to Muslims (e.g., the constant harassment of Muslims under a draconian law or the non-recognition of Islamic family law with respect to marital and divorce issues). Such feebleness indicates that either your organization lacks a national following, or that your leadership is ineffectual, or that your membership is at best effete and unmotivated. The bottom-line is the following: If your organization is not providing value to its constituency, your constituency may not feel any need to reciprocate with financial, moral, and other support. Why should your members do anything for you if you cannot do anything for them?

2. **The Question of Rarity**: Is your strength one which few organizations in your domain or niche have access to? Is your organization one that can lead and accomplish projects that no other similar organizations or individual can? What is unique and distinctive about your strength?

3. **The Question of Imitability**: Can other organizations that lack this strength build it up without a major investment in resources? Such organizations as CAIR, IMRC, and Savola were not built overnight. Their leaders and founders spent a lot of time, money and effort assembling the right configuration of people and assets, shaping the right organizational culture with appropriate norms and values, and building worthwhile inter-organizational relationships. Trying

SWOT ANALYSIS

to imitate an organization that is already established within a niche means overcoming barriers to entry (e.g., name recognition, capitalization, access to potential donors/investors, and location). Even when an organization has access to a lot of assets and can penetrate a niche, it may still fail because it cannot surpass an established competitor's learning curve quickly enough to provide products or services on the scale that it needs to survive. There are many examples of Islamic banks that failed because their founders underestimated the difficulties of imitating a rival's strengths. Even when they had the financial resources, they did not have the human assets, experience, and credibility required to run such an enterprise. One defunct Islamic bank I know of was literally run from its president's front shirt pocket. He was an honest man, but he did not understand basic financial accounting and economics. As a result, he ended up in jail when there was a run on the bank, and it collapsed.

4. **The Question of Organization**: Does your organization have the capabilities (viz., structure, alliances, and policies) in place to use this strength to its full potential? Having a strength does not mean that it can be deployed effectively. At the battle of Yarmuk, the 200,000-man Byzantine army lost to the 40,000-man Muslim army because they literally got in each other's way during the battle. Similarly, Islamic organizations that were nimble when they were still young and small can become oceans of mind-numbing bureaucracy as they mature and expand. Instead of larger size being a strength, it actually becomes a major weakness when coupled with a poorly designed structure and conflicting rules and standard operating procedures. Unless an appropriate structure is coupled with your organization's strategy, any strength it may have can easily be dissipated through disorganization.

In contrast to organizational strengths, organizational weaknesses are typically something that the organization lacks, is relatively ineffective at, or a situation that somehow hampers it. With reference to the above list of strengths, organizational weaknesses include a lack of human resources and competencies, an inability to own or control key assets, a poor reputation, a weak corporate culture, and/or the absence of cooperative relationships. Table 3.1 lists potential strengths and weaknesses that Islamic organizations may face.

SWOT ANALYSIS

Table 3.1
SWOT Analysis – Internal Audit

Potential Strengths	Potential Weaknesses
Financial stability backed up by a good stream of assets	Poor debt/asset ratio
A national reputation associated with a growing membership or customer base	A no-name organization or declining reputation
Strong corporate values	A weak corporate culture
Strategically located facilities that are easily accessible	A lack of facilities or dilapidated physical assets
An effective leadership	No clear leader or a poor leadership succession plan
Great intellectual capital	Copycat
A superior quality product or service	Easily imitable or low quality product or service
A clear, disciplined strategy	No strategy or fuzzy strategy that is unevenly implemented
A motivated, unified workforce or membership	A lethargic, internally fragmented workforce or membership

Strengths can sometimes be weaknesses just as opportunities can be threats, or vice-versa.

Note that strengths and weaknesses are relative to one's competitors within the same or adjacent domains or business areas. Often, a factor that an Islamic organization views as a strength may be viewed by an outside observer as a weakness if one of its rivals can do better. For example, a leading national Islamic organization used to be very proud of its membership size. But when the number of its registered members was expressed as a percentage of the nation's Muslim population, it was far less than one thousandth of one percent (.001)! You can engage in self-deception by calling something a strength, but rivals and external stakeholders do not have these same perceptual biases and will correctly assess that "strength" as a weakness.

Cultural Audit

While analyzing your organization's strengths and weaknesses, work to uncover the values and assumptions that guide your employees, members, and key stakeholders. These values and assumptions underlie the organization's decision-making process and, if they are not congruent with the strategic plan being developed, they may represent an organizational weakness and hinder the planning and implementation processes. For the purposes of this book, a value within the context of organizational culture is defined as "the collective principle and ideal which guides the thoughts and actions of an individual, or a group of individuals,"[9] and a core assumption is defined as a fact or statement taken for granted or a "theory-in-use that is neither questioned nor debated."[10]

In performing a cultural audit, the SPC must distinguish between personal and organizational values and assumptions. The organization's key decision-makers must be forthright about their personal values and recognize that the organization may have different values. For example, Savola is guided by such internal values as `*azm* (resolve), *iqtida* (apprenticeship), *itqan* (relentless pursuit of perfection) and *tawadu* (humility), as well as by such external values as *ihsan al-dhan* (trusting) and *mu'azarah* (caring to help). Similarly, Southwest Airlines prizes its customer friendliness, whereas Dupont emphasizes safety, ethics, respect for people, and environmental stewardship.

A cultural audit is critical, because values can represent an important source of competitive advantage and be a strength, as they have been for Savola and Southwest Airlines. On the other hand, a weak culture can be a major obstacle to rethinking an organization's strategy and implementing key changes.

> SWOT should also include a cultural audit.

Scanning the External Environment

When scanning its external environment, an organization focuses on potential opportunities and threats related to current or prospective customers, suppliers, rivals or competitors, and partners.[11] As Barney and Hesterly indicate, the external analysis builds on the internal analysis and tells you what the organization *should* do.[12]

Opportunities, which originate from the organization's external environment, can include any potential areas for growth, technological change, or demographic trends (see table 3.2). Note that even when an external opportunity is rated very high in attractiveness, you may still decide not to channel resources toward it, for as Spulber indicates, it may not match your organization's strengths or may not be right for your community's stage of development.[13] For example, a small American Muslim community learned that a very large and spacious building was on the market. It had everything: a large hall that could be converted into a prayer hall, an indoor gym/basketball court, a swimming pool, lodging facilities with numerous rooms, a large parking lot, and was located close to a park. The community's leaders realized that they simply did not have the financial resources to maintain this building, even if the community were somehow able to purchase it through fundraising. The community's current and projected sizes were below the critical mass needed to support such a large center over the next 20 years. Thus, despite the attractiveness of the opportunity, the leadership decided not to purchase the property. Here is a case of the community rejecting something that looked very appealing. Had its leaders bought this property and then been unable to remodel or maintain it, this building could have drained much needed resources and hurt the community's very viability.

In contrast, as shown in table 3.2, external threats are agents, factors, or trends that pose a danger to the organization.

> The external analysis tells you what your organization should do, and builds on the internal analysis.

Table 3.2
SWOT Analysis – External Environment Scan

Potential Opportunities	Potential Threats
Growing Muslim community	New crop of rivals and imitators providing new/better services and products
New technologies enabling new ways of delivering da`wah and zakah donation and distribution services	New technologies making it easier to vilify Islam and to create a negative and harsh public image
Tapping into financial aid sources available to minorities or low-income families	Legislation restricting fundraising and sending funds to Muslim causes
Establishing strategic alliances	Increased scrutiny from external stakeholders because of alliances
Developing new customer services	Obsolete customer services
Acquiring rivals that possess unique competencies	Potential takeover or ban
Interfaith initiatives	Increased isolation from other faith-based communities

SWOT ANALYSIS

Worksheets nos. 3 through 6 (Appendix A, pp. 166-169) are designed to guide you through the SWOT analysis. I will discuss the ranking column in these worksheets shortly.

Prioritizing the SWOT

After listing your organization's strengths, weaknesses, opportunities and threats, rank each category within itself. In other words, rank strengths from "most important" to "least important," weaknesses from "most critical" to "least critical," opportunities from "most attractive" to "least attractive," and threats from "most serious" to "least serious." There are multiple ways of doing this balloting process. Worksheets nos. 3 through 6 (Appendix A) consist of several forms that you can use to list all of your SPC's strengths, weaknesses, opportunities, and threats. After doing this, ask the committee to collapse the complete list into a more concise one and to rank it. There are two methods of calculating ranking:

After listing your organization's strengths, rank your strengths from most important to least important. Do a similar ranking for your weaknesses, opportunities and threats.

First Method

Photocopy the list for each SPC member and have him/her rate (in secret) each strength, weakness, opportunity, and threat as suggested by worksheets nos. 3 through 6. Next, ask an assistant to enter the resulting ranked data into a spreadsheet, calculate each strength's mean rank, and then rank the strengths from the most important (strongest) to the least important (weakest). Do the same for weaknesses, opportunities, and threats.

Second Method

Use green dot balloting, a technique that is both simple and fun.

Green dot balloting is a simple and fun technique to facilitate the ranking process.

- Before conducting the SWOT exercise, purchase about 25 sheets of sticky green dots (about 40 per sheet with each dot being about .5 inch in diameter). Clearly, the number of sheets you need depends upon the number of participants at the retreat (about 40 dots per participant), and the number of strengths, weaknesses, opportunities, and threats that are generated during the SWOT analysis. You will also need a pad of easel-sized sheets of paper and a roll of masking (or regular) tape that will not damage the walls. 3M makes a large easel pad size of Post-it note sheets; however, these are somewhat expensive. Draw two

SWOT ANALYSIS

- columns on your easel pad, a wider column on the left and a narrower column on the right.
- Start with the strengths. Ask each participant to read his/her top two strengths and have a volunteer with good handwriting write these (listed as A, B, etc.) in the wider left-hand column. Next, ask each participant to read his/her top two strengths, provided that nobody repeats a strength that is already listed. Once each easel sheet is filled up, tear it off and have your volunteer tape it on the wall. Continue until all strengths have been listed without any duplication. You should now have several sheets taped to the wall, each one of which lists your organization's strengths in the wider left-hand column.
- Have your volunteer distribute to each participant between 1/5 to 1/3 as many dots as there are listed strengths. The same amount of dots should be given to each participant. In other words, if there are 24 strengths listed and you have decided to give 1/3 as many dots as there are listed strengths, each participant should receive 8 green dots.
- Ask each participant to allocate his/her dots to the strengths listed. Each person must do so silently and write on the dot the letter of the strength he/she is ranking. Let's say you gave 8 dots to each participant. If he/she were to rank strength B as "most important," followed by strength D and strength A, he/she would write B on 4 dots, D on 3 dots, and A on the remaining dot.
- Once each participant is done, he/she cannot change his/her mind. Ask the participants to get up and, in an orderly manner, stick the appropriate number of dots in the right-hand column next to the relevant strength. Your easel pad should look like exhibit A.
- Once everybody is done, a quick visual count will reveal the rank of each strength. It may now be possible to group together those ranked strengths that are close in meaning in order to provide a tighter set. In exhibit A, your strengths are to be ranked in the following order based on the number of dots attached to them: D (18), B (10), C (8), and A (7).

SWOT ANALYSIS

Exhibit A
Sample Easel Pad Sheet after All Participants Have Voted with Their Dots

---

A. We have a large Muslim community	Ⓐ Ⓐ Ⓐ Ⓐ Ⓐ Ⓐ Ⓐ
B. Many professionals live in our community	Ⓑ Ⓑ Ⓑ Ⓑ Ⓑ Ⓑ Ⓑ Ⓑ Ⓑ Ⓑ
C. We have excellent relations with other faith-based communities	Ⓒ Ⓒ Ⓒ Ⓒ Ⓒ Ⓒ Ⓒ Ⓒ
D. We have a full-time Islamic school	Ⓓ Ⓓ Ⓓ Ⓓ Ⓓ Ⓓ Ⓓ Ⓓ Ⓓ Ⓓ Ⓓ Ⓓ Ⓓ Ⓓ Ⓓ Ⓓ Ⓓ

- Repeat the same voting process for assessing the organization's weaknesses, opportunities, and threats.

The rationale for this ranking process is that your organization may not be uniformly strong across all areas. Each organization has distinctive core competencies in which it outshines its competitors and should capitalize on them. Similarly, your weaknesses, opportunities, and threats are not uniformly weighted; there are some weaknesses where you are more at risk, some opportunities that are more promising, and some threats that are more dire. Ideally, a value-maximizing goal for an Islamic organization is to match its most important strength to its most attractive opportunity, given situational parameters. The rationale for secret balloting is to preempt flaws in group decision-making processes, such as groupthink,[14] risky shift, and even polarization.

Collaborator Analysis

Competitors can also be collaborators.

While doing your external environmental scanning, distinguish between external stakeholders with whom you could build a strategic alliance (a collaborator) and those with whom you will have to constantly compete (a competitor). Collaborative strategies are now an important part of the business and the nonprofit worlds.[15] For example, Dell may currently compete with Sony, but for quite a while Sony manufactured Dell's best-selling notebooks. In analyzing various potential collaborators, be aware that the ensuing collaborative relationship may only extend to a specific product, program, or activity. To protect proprietary know-how, you may wish to compartmentalize your activities. The core issue is one of synergy and whether the collaborative relationship adds any value.

Before initiating any collaborative ventures, delimit the nature of the area of cooperation. Try to gauge how your service or product benchmarks against theirs, as well as the advantages and disadvantages of working jointly with them, the length of the relationship, and the conditions under which either party can extend or terminate the relationship. It is a good idea to have the relationship formally written up, as Islam suggests, and signed by the leaders of both organizations before initiating it. Doing so will enable you to avoid unpleasant surprises and feeling a potential sense of betrayal if the relationship does not work out.

Competitor Analysis

> Competitor analysis allows you to obtain a deep understanding of your rival's strategies, objectives, assumptions and capabilities in order to forecast and anticipate his future behavior.

Conducting a competitor analysis enables you to gather intelligence about your rival's strategies, objectives, assumptions, and capabilities in order to predict potential future behavior. From Caesar to Khalid ibn Walid to Salahuddin, all great generals have been characterized by their ability to go beyond the intelligence gathered and see through the enemy's plans. Listen to Khalid ibn Walid's advice to his commander Abu Ubayda, as the overwhelming forces of Byzantium were gathering to annihilate the Muslims:

> Know, O Commander, that if you stay at this place, you will be helping the enemy against you. In Caesarea, which is not far from Jabiya, there are 40,000 Romans under Constantine, son of Heraclius. I advise you to move from here and place Azra behind you and be on the Yarmuk. Thus it would be easier for the Caliph to send reinforcements, and ahead of you there would be a large plain, suitable for the charge of cavalry.[16]

In contrast to the grim indecisiveness of Abu Ubayda and other Muslim generals, Khalid was able to visualize the whole battlefield, the enemy's position, and the need to relocate so that the Muslim army could both attack using one of its core strengths (its cavalry) and receive reinforcements.

3
SWOT ANALYSIS

Just as Khalid used intelligence to outthink his enemy, so too Harvard's Michael Porter has introduced the idea of using competitor analysis for organizational leaders who wish to outthink and preempt potential competitors.[17]

The importance of this analysis depends on the structure of the industry or domain in which your Islamic organization exists. In general, a competitor analysis is undertaken to:

- Forecast and map out your competitors' future strategies and initiatives,
- Anticipate their potential reactions to your own organization's strategic moves, and
- Assess how their behavior can be rechanneled to benefit your organization.

A competitor analysis consists of four inputs: the competitor's current strategy, objectives, assumptions about the industry, and capabilities. Assessing the competitor's current strategy involves seeking answers to one key question: How is your rival competing at present? To find out, look at the official pronouncements of its president/CEO and at all official publications, reports, and other public documents. However, you will need to distinguish between what Mintzberg calls an *intended* versus a *realized* strategy.[18] What an organization intends to do may be different from what it actually does. Organizations are also more likely to divulge their official initiatives (*public* strategies) than their real intentions (*private* strategies). To guess through the fog of all these strategy variants, focus on any changes in your competitor's strategy, for these are what may reveal his/her real strategy.

When identifying your competitor's current objectives, try to answer the following three questions:

a) What are his/her current goals with respect to profitability and market (membership) share?
b) Does current performance meet current goals?
c) How are his/her goals likely to change in the future?

To the extent that your competitor is more concerned about meeting the bottom-line numbers, he/she may not care whether you are reaching into his/her niche or domain. Your competitor is more likely to leave you alone if his/her business is performing well and meeting its current goals comfortably. As long as current goals are being met, your competitor will assume that his/her business or organization model is working effectively.

> What an organization intends to do may differ from what it actually does.

He/she will hold on to his/her "industry recipes" or industry-wide beliefs about the factors that drive success and, as a result, will be less likely to adjust his/her goals, strategies, and objectives to challenge you.

Finally, gauge your competitor's capabilities carefully to ascertain his/her principal strengths and weaknesses. At this point, I suggest that you do a SWOT of each major competitor, for the extent to which a competitor threatens your organization's industry or domain position depends upon his/her capabilities. If your competitor has a major strength in an area in which you do not, it would be unwise for you to mount a challenge. Your SWOT will reveal his/her weaknesses and, hence, potential areas in which you can make an inroad.

Once you are done with your competitor analysis, you can more accurately forecast your competitor's future strategy shifts. Of course, such shifts are not idiosyncratic, for they require an understanding of forces that are likely to provoke a change in strategy. Clearly, such external jolts as the 9/11 tragedy, a change in consumer preferences, a tsunami, internal pressures (e.g., failure to achieve current market-share targets), or internal factional conflict are examples of strategy-shifting forces.

After 9/11, for example, many Islamic organizations realized that they needed to dialogue with members of other-faith based communities to allay their misunderstandings and fears about Islam and Muslims. Mosques in North America opened their doors for the first time to non-Muslims. As a result, many Muslims made new friends and became more involved in their local community, instead of perpetuating the awkward aloofness that had existed until then.

Worksheet #7 (Appendix A, p. 170) will enable your organization to assess exactly who its potential competitors may be and what their likely impact will be on your organization and its niche and/or domain.

Driving Forces

Driving forces represent the top three or four primary causes underlying industry and competitive conditions.

To understand the external opportunities and threats facing your organization, the SPC must identify the forces that drive the relevant industry or niche, for these represent "the major underlying causes of changing industry and competitive conditions."[19] Identifying these forces and taking appropriate steps to plan and implement your organization's strategic plan is critical for long-term effectiveness. Examples of driving forces in one's industry include changes in who buys/uses the product or service (e.g., older vs. younger customers, families vs. singles, immigrant or indigenous Muslims), product or service innovation (e.g., new instruments in the

SWOT ANALYSIS

Islamic finance industry), technological change (doing *da`wah* via the Internet rather than face-to-face), the entry or exit of major organizations (e.g., the exodus of Muslim relief agencies after 9/11), changes in cost and efficiency (e-mail vs. regular mail), and changes in government policy (the U.S. Patriot Act and subsequent negative side-effects). Such driving forces change the dynamics faced by Islamic organizations or businesses and need to be taken into account when developing your strategic plan.

When assessing driving forces, the SPC should scan a broad array of political, religious, social, economic, technological, and environmental factors that are likely to influence the Islamic organization or business. Since many external events can affect the organization's industry or domain quite strongly, focus on the top four or five driving forces and try to track trends rather than discrete, unrelated blips. For example, a continuous pattern of harassing Muslims (e.g., burning down mosques, desecrating the Qur'an or Islamic cemeteries, loss of jobs, verbal abuse, physical assaults, murder, and so on) indicates a trend, whereas a couple of isolated and random hate crimes signify no more than a blip.

CHAPTER 4

DEVELOPING VISION AND MISSION STATEMENTS

يَٰٓأَيُّهَا ٱلَّذِينَ ءَامَنُواْ ٱسْتَعِينُواْ بِٱلصَّبْرِ وَٱلصَّلَوٰةِ إِنَّ ٱللَّهَ مَعَ ٱلصَّٰبِرِينَ ۝

O you who believe! Seek help with patient perseverance and prayer, for Allah is with those who patiently persevere. (Qur'an, 2:153)

> A vision statement is future-oriented and outlines what an organization wishes to become. A mission statement describes what the organization needs to do *now* to realize its vision.

Thinking strategically about your organization's future and long-term direction, as well as its identity and domain, is hard and can easily become nebulous. A vision and a mission statement can provide focus during the strategic planning and implementation processes.[1] A vision statement is future-oriented and outlines, in very broad terms, what the organization wishes to become. A mission statement, on the other hand, describes the organization's *raison d'être*, its self-concept, and what it needs to do now to realize its vision. Frequently, the mission statement will list, either explicitly or implicitly, the values by which the organization abides.

Here, we note Prophet Muhammad's vision at Khandaq, where he outlined the Ummah's future direction. In answering Salman's question about the three lightning sparks toward the south, north, and east, the Prophet said:

> *Did you see them, Salman? By the light of the first, I saw the castles of Yemen; by the light of the second, I saw the castles of Syria; by the light of the third, I saw the white palace of Kisra at Mada'in. Through the first has Allah opened up to me the Yemen; through the second has He opened up to me Syria and the West, and through the third, the East.*[2]

This vision at Khandaq is different from typical organizational visions, for it was divinely inspired. Yet, it has continued to inspire the Ummah through good and bad times, has elicited the Muslims' enthusiasm over the centuries, and continues to guide us.

Defining the Vision Statement

Defining a vision statement is a must. Take time to outline your organization's strategic vision, because it will preempt current and future leaders from acting without considering the general, long-term direction in which they wish to take the organization. By pressing the decision makers to think long-term and consider overall trends, a vision enables leaders to be proactive rather than reactive. As you get ready to map out the future direction of your Islamic organization or business, take the time to pray *salat al-istikhara* (described on page 158) and ask Allah for guidance. Enacting the vision will require faith, commitment, and patience.

> Pray *salat al-istikhara* as you work on the future direction of your Islamic organization.

The leader's vision does not need to be detailed or follow a standard format. In fact, depending on the leader, the nature of the organization and the internal or external environment, it can be rather idiosyncratic. Sometimes, the vision focuses on a specific issue that the organization is trying to address: the educational needs of Muslim children, the erosion of civil rights, the media's defamation of Islam and Muslims, interfaith activities, and so on. The vision often charts a bold new direction: to become the medium for *da`wah* in the country where the organization is located. Regardless of its content, the vision guides the participants' efforts and proclaims to all what the organization intends to become,[3] with Allah's permission. It acts as a magnet to attract the public and other external stakeholders to its activities, galvanizes organizational participants, and provides an end for which to aim.

DEVELOPING VISION AND MISSION STATEMENTS

In delineating a vision statement, use worksheet 8 (Appendix A, p. 171) to guide your SPC. You will need to ask a number of questions[4]:

1. What domain (i.e., area, field, industry, niche) are we in now?
2. In what domain do we want to be in the future?
3. What do our stakeholders want now and in the future?
4. Who will be our future competitors/partners?
5. Should our scope of operations be local, regional, national, international, global, or transnational?
6. What kind of position (e.g., leader, small player) do we want to achieve in our domain?

When wording a vision statement, remember to keep it simple and concise so that when it is broadcast to the intended audience, it arouses the hoped-for dedication and enthusiasm. On 28 August 1963, on the steps of the Lincoln Memorial (Washington, DC), Dr. Martin Luther King enunciated in eloquent and moving words the dream of the whole Afro-American community:

> *I have a dream that one day this nation will rise up and live out the true meaning of its creed. We hold these truths to be self-evident that all men are created equal.*
>
> *I have a dream that one day on the red hills of Georgia the sons of former slaves and the sons of former slave owners will be able to sit down together at the table of brotherhood.*
>
> *I have a dream that one day even the state of Mississippi, a state sweltering with the heat of oppression, will be transformed into an oasis of freedom and justice.*
>
> *I have a dream that my four little children will one day live in a nation where they will not be judged by the color of their skin but by the content of their character.*[5]

A vision is intuitive and idealistic. Drawing from organizational experience and history, as well as from knowledge search, it focuses on possibilities rather than probabilities[6] and represents "a statement of destination" or an idealized future state that the organization wishes to reach. The vision statements of several leading organizations and corporations are included in illustration capsule 1.

A vision statement is not the same as a mission statement. A vision focuses on the future – what we wish to become. A mission concerns

DEVELOPING VISION AND MISSION STATEMENTS

itself with the present – what we need to accomplish now to bring us closer to realizing our vision. A mission statement describes an organization's *raison d'être* (current purpose) as well as its current capabilities, values, and philosophy. In other words, the vision shapes the mission.

Illustration Capsule 1

Examples of Vision Statements

AMNESTY INTERNATIONAL
Amnesty International's vision is of a world in which every person enjoys all of the human rights enshrined in the Universal Declaration of Human Rights and other international human rights standards.

SAVOLA GROUP
To build a leading publicly listed diversified investment group in the Middle East based on Savola's "Balanced Way" corporate culture.

COUNCIL OF AMERICAN ISLAMIC RELATIONS (CAIR)
To be a leading advocate for justice and mutual understanding.

ISLAMIC SOCIETY OF NORTH AMERICA
To be an exemplary and unifying Islamic organization in North America that contributes to the betterment of the Muslim community and society at large.

ISLAMIC MEDICAL ASSOCIATION OF NORTH AMERICA
To become the recognized leader in national and global healthcare, guided by Islamic values.

ONTARIO FEDERATION OF TEACHING PARENTS
We envision universal acknowledgement and acceptance of home-based education as a viable educational model. OFTP will be recognized as a significant and valuable authority and advocate for home-based education in Ontario.

ISLAMIC CENTER OF LONG ISLAND
To be a center of excellence for developing and sustaining a progressive, vibrant Islamic community and a nurturing environment for the society at large.

Inspiring a Shared Vision

When developing a vision, you, as the leader, need to actively involve your members and strengthen their commitment to it. After investigating how effective leaders inspire their organization, Kouzes and Posner found out that visions involving the people who will be responsible for implementing them tend to be more motivating.[7] In other words, leaders can stir their members to action by inspiring a shared vision. *Shura* can be instrumental both in developing and in imparting the vision. According to Bennis, leaders are effective when they focus commitment to a vision and communicate that vision.[8]

> A Muslim leader must share his/her vision with his/her followers if it is to motivate them.

The core idea here is that the leader's vision needs to be shared by the organization's members if they are to increase their commitment to its implementation.[9] When other organizational participants adopt the vision, they begin to see it as part of their own agenda and so champion it and spread it to others. To help others share the vision, leaders must embrace it and articulate it in powerful and emotive language.

Developing a vision does not mean that all of the necessary steps have been delineated. A vision focuses on the desired end state, not on how it will be accomplished. In fact, the leader may not wish to clarify this process since the mere act of having the participants figure out how to fulfill the vision may make them feel even more empowered and motivated.

When you, as the leader, spoon-feed your organization, or when the vision is not shared by everyone, the process of envisioning may suffer from several defects, as depicted in table 4.

Egocentricism. An organization's vision should not be limited to the interests of special factions, groups, or nationalities, for Islam opposes '*asabiyyah* (putting the needs of one's group or clan ahead of those of the community). Since the Prophet stressed the importance of competence and did not appoint one of his relatives as his immediate successor, Islam also opposes nepotism. To avoid a self-centered approach, the leader needs to involve as many members as possible, provided that they have the appropriate expertise, in developing the organization's vision. To ensure their commitment to the vision, the *shura* process must involve at least the *ahl ar-raie* (those competent to participate in the decision) as an integral part.

The Resource Gap. Often, the leader may underestimate the resources needed to realize the vision. This may lead to an overstretched current capacity and less organizational effectiveness. To avoid this mistake, the leader may use the SWOT analysis of his/her organization to anchor its vision statement.

Table 4
Sources of Defective Vision

Egocentricism	The vision reflects a preoccupation with the leader's personal needs rather than with those of the Ummah or the local community.
Resource Gap	The president has miscalculated the resources needed to realize the vision.
Closed-system Perspective	The president has misunderstood or underestimated the impact of external environmental forces on the vision. Hence, the vision is rigid and inflexible.
Groupthink	The president may use *shura* to consult others in defining the vision, but all members think alike and thus suffer from tunnel vision.

Undertaking a SWOT analysis (see chapter 3) enables the leader to assess the resource gap between the resources that the organization controls and those that it needs in order to tap into key external opportunities or counter external threats. By carrying out a SWOT analysis in conjunction with the process of envisioning, the community's leader and the SPC will develop a realistic vision.

The Closed System Perspective. A leader who maps out the organization's path without taking into account what is happening on the outside is acting as though his/her organization is a closed system. One Islamic organization fell into this trap. For years, it excelled by monitoring, anticipating, and adapting to its external environment. But later on, when it became somewhat disconnected from external events due to its increased size and promotion of insiders to leadership positions, its services no longer addressed the changing needs of the Muslim and non-Muslim community. It has been in the throes of a long agony ever since.

Groupthink. The *shura* process may be deliberately distorted. If

DEVELOPING VISION AND MISSION STATEMENTS

you, as the leader, surround yourself with yes-men or yes-women, the outcome will naturally validate your own decisions. If this is your goal, why should you even bother with *shura*? This drive for consensus and simultaneous suppression of dissent leads to *groupthink*.[10] You must constantly watch out for this dysfunctional result by ensuring that no consulted member is afraid to voice his/her opinion, even if it contradicts everybody else's and challenges your own perspective. Imam Ali stressed this principle in his letter to Malik al-Ashtar al-Nukai:

> *Gather honest, truthful, and pious people around you as your companions and friends. Train them not to flatter you, and not to seek your favor by false praises. [...] Try to realize that a ruler can create goodwill in the minds of his subjects. He can make them faithful and sincere only when he is kind and considerate, when he reduces their troubles and difficulties, when he does not oppress or tyrannize them, and when he never asks for things beyond their capacities.*[11]

In other words, the leader should make sure that members of the board of directors or board of advisors or the SPC are not seeking his/her approval gratuitously or acting as his/her clones.

As one of my mentors once said, negative feedback should be treasured because it indicates where one can improve. Positive feedback, on the other hand, only reinforces the status quo. Listen to any feedback, whether positive or negative. Once a person stood up in a public meeting and told Umar to fear [and respect] Allah. The audience tried to stop him, but Umar said: "Let him speak. He is free to give his opinion. If people do not give their opinions they are useless, and if we (the rulers) do not listen to them we are useless." The above quotation from Imam Ali also discusses how you can ensure that your followers are not self-serving.

Finally, when defining your vision and mission statements, transcend the "curse of competence" discussed earlier.[12] Several national Islamic organizations have stumbled because they accomplished their initial mission so well that they decided to branch out into areas where they lacked competence. In addition, the previous standards of excellence that these Islamic institutions and organizations had to meet often are no longer applicable, since key stakeholders now expect better and more relevant services. Just because your organization has done something

4

DEVELOPING VISION AND MISSION STATEMENTS

well for years does not mean that it will always be good – or the best – at what it does. Service and product quality are never-ending quests. Do not limp forward on your laurels. As your organization defines its vision and mission statements, it will need to benchmark itself against the best and reject the low standards of performance that many Islamic organizations seem to accept as the norm.

Using a SWOT analysis to guide how you formulate your vision and mission statement will enable your organization to understand its true distinctive competencies and what it *can* be best at. For an Islamic non-profit organization, focus on *those areas within the context of your vision and mission statements about which your membership can be passionate*. Every Islamic organization dreams about being the best, but most of them lack the discipline needed to determine with *self-less lucidity what they can be best at* and lack the will to do whatever it takes to transform hopes into reality. You do not need to be in a "hot" area to be excellent. Given your core competencies, be the best in setting up endowments (*awqaf*), selling Islamic books on the Internet, running soup kitchens, engaging in interfaith dialogue, providing shelters to abused women, or developing an Islamic Sunday school curricula. Pick one niche and excel in it, for Muslims are expected to achieve excellence as part of their *ihsan*.

Defining the Mission Statement

Building upon the vision statement, a mission statement broadly outlines the organization's purpose and serves as its guiding concept: who we are and what we do. As Abrahams sums it up, "[a] vision is something to be pursued whereas a mission is something to be accomplished."[13] Defining a mission statement is critical. In fact, Covey states that "[an] organizational mission statement – one that truly reflects the deep shared vision and values of everyone within that organization – creates a great unity and tremendous commitment. It creates in people's hearts and minds a frame of reference, a set of criteria or guidelines, by which they will govern themselves. [...] They have bought into the changeless core of what the organization is about."[14]

In developing its mission statement, your Islamic organization – whether for-profit or not-for-profit – needs to recall humanity's core mission, as stated in:

قُلْ إِنَّ صَلَاتِي وَنُسُكِي وَمَحْيَايَ وَمَمَاتِي لِلَّهِ رَبِّ ٱلْعَٰلَمِينَ ۝

DEVELOPING VISION AND MISSION STATEMENTS

Say: "Truly, my prayer and my service of sacrifice, my life and my death, are (all) for Allah, the Cherisher of the Worlds."
(Qur'an, 6:162)

Here, Allah reminds humanity of its purpose for being. As all of our actions are ultimately done to serve Our Creator, they therefore must correlate with the moral and ethical parameters He has outlined for us. The mission of an Islamic business should not be stated in terms of making a profit, for profit results from what the business does. Therefore, it is more of an objective than a *raison d'être* of the organization itself.[15] As George indicates, companies that dedicate themselves to profits and maximizing shareholder value will ultimately fail, whereas companies that pursue their mission in a consistent and unrelenting manner will create value for their shareholders far beyond their expectations.[16] An excellent example is Medtronics Corporation, which George, during his tenure as CEO, brought from $1.5 billion to $60 billion once he stopped worrying about shareholder value and focused on his company's mission.

When defining your organization's mission statement, use worksheet #9 (Appendix A, p. 172). The mission statement must meet three criteria.[17] First, it should reflect who its key customers are. Customers are not all the same, especially if the organization functions in multiple segments, such as gender (women vs. men), age (young vs. adult), and geographical location (the United States vs. Canada). By understanding which customer(s) it serves, your organization will be more responsive to their needs.

Second, the mission statement needs to provide a clear view of what your organization is trying to accomplish for its customers. In defining these services, the SPC must strike a balance between being too broad and too narrow. Peters and Waterman describe as excellent organizations those that "stick to the knitting,"[18] while Levitt stresses the idea that an organization should avoid *strategic myopia*.[19] For example, instead of seeing themselves as being in the railroad industry and myopically positioning themselves in a narrow, dying industry, firms that ship by train should have seen themselves as being in the broader, growing transportation industry.[20] Misunderstanding what industry they served caused many of these train-related firms to fail at a later date.

> In defining your mission statement, you must maintain a balance between 'sticking to the knitting' and engaging in 'strategic myopia'.

4
DEVELOPING VISION AND MISSION STATEMENTS

Figure 3
Simple Value Chain for a Not-for-Profit Organization

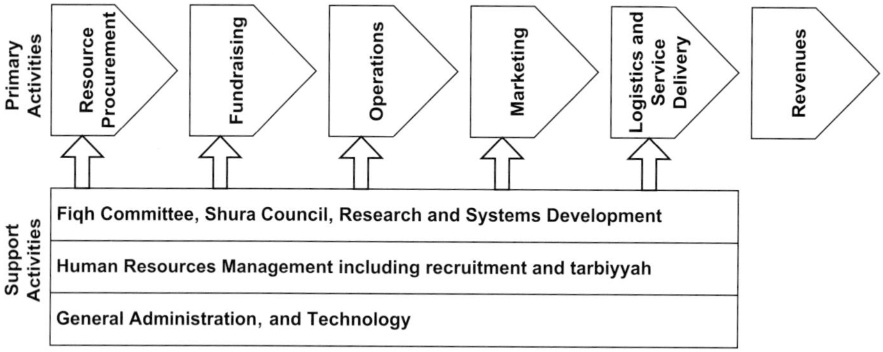

Primary Activities: Resource Procurement → Fundraising → Operations → Marketing → Logistics and Service Delivery → Revenues

Support Activities:
- Fiqh Committee, Shura Council, Research and Systems Development
- Human Resources Management including recruitment and tarbiyyah
- General Administration, and Technology

[Reprinted and modified with permission of the Free Press, a Division of Simon & Schuster Adult Publishing Group, from *Competitive Advantage: Creating and Sustaining Superior Performance* by Michael Porter. Copyright (c) 1985, 1998 by Michael E. Porter. All rights reserved.]

> A Muslim organization's value chain segments its primary activities into a sequential chain ranging from procurement of resources to providing support after the product/service is delivered to its key customer.

When it comes to serving customer needs, however defined, organizations also differ in their center of gravity. To explain this statement, consider the concept of a *value chain* (see figure 3). An organization's or a business' value chain separates its activities into a sequential chain ranging from procurement of resources through production to selling the product or providing a service, and beyond.[21] Other activities (e.g., staffing, research and systems development, and administration) are viewed as activities that support those in the value chain.

In relation to their value chain and which component(s) they emphasize, Islamic organizations can be considered as specialized, partly integrated, or fully integrated. This does not mean that they neglect the other activities in their value chain; rather, they differentiate themselves from other Islamic organizations and potential competitors by developing core competencies in specific activities. For example, IMRC specializes and focuses primarily on one link: prompt service delivery of emergency relief and charity. It does not manufacture emergency tents, train future imams, or engage in Islamic banking. Rather, when an emergency occurs, it pulls together already existing resources to serve those in need.

Other organizations are partly integrated and develop competencies in more than one link, such as in resource procurement (aided by research), marketing, logistics, and service delivery. For instance, CAIR often tracks and gathers data about discriminatory behavior against Muslims (research), launches an intensive advertising campaign (marketing), and then publicizes this data or advocates on behalf of the victims (logistics and service delivery). The last group of organizations is fully integrated, for they emphasize all of the links in the value chain. Thus, they function like a one-stop shopping center within their niche. The International Institute of Islamic Thought (IIIT) receives and reviews manuscripts (resource procurement), publishes those that meet certain criteria (operations and outbound logistics), and then sells them both directly as well as through vendors (marketing, sales, and revenue collection).

Hence, *a mission statement will reflect the center of gravity unique to the organization*. Based on your value chain, are you specialized in one activity (IMRC), do all of the activities within your area or niche (IIIT), or do some of the activities within your area or niche (CAIR) when serving your customers' needs?

Third, the mission statement needs to clarify its *strategic intent* to show just how distinctive its products or services are. Specifically, when determining how to differentiate its product or service (e.g., quality, service, price, and features), an organization is deciding how it will set itself apart from the competition. For example, if you are a small Islamic publishing house, you can publish a book cheaper than any of your competitors. However, the quality of the job and the paper used may not be as good. In this case, you are differentiating your product on the basis of price, not quality. Your mission statement should reflect how you intend to differentiate your organization, or its product or service, from potential competitors. The strategic intent can be stated explicitly for your organizational participants' benefit. For example, the strategic intent of NASA's Apollo space program was to "put a man on the moon before the Soviets." The strategic intent can also be meant as a message to external stakeholders. Here note the example of Abu Bakr, who, fighting those new Muslims who refused to pay their zakah, told all stakeholders that he was determined to preserve at any cost the integrity of Allah's message as revealed to Muhammad.

To illustrate how these three criteria work, look at how we have broken down the mission statement of Ameen Housing Coop: "To enable members to make secure and profitable investments and/or purchase homes in an Islamic manner."[22]

4
DEVELOPING VISION AND MISSION STATEMENTS

Illustration Capsule 2
How the Three Criteria of a Mission Statement Work Together

Key market:	Members of Ameen Housing Coop
Contribution:	Secure and profitable investments and/or home purchase
Distinction:	In an Islamic manner

Thompson, Gamble, and Strickland suggest that the following questions may help members define the mission statement[23]:

- Who are we?
- What are the needs that we exist to meet, or what problems do we exist to address?
- What do we do to recognize, anticipate, and respond to these needs or problems?
- How should we respond to our key stakeholders?
- What are our philosophy, values, and culture?
- What makes us distinctive or unique?

Illustration Capsule 3 (a) lists some effective mission statements.

Illustration Capsule 3 (a)
Examples of Mission Statements

AMNESTY INTERNATIONAL
To undertake research and action focused on preventing and ending grave abuses of the rights to physical and mental integrity, freedom of conscience and expression, and freedom from discrimination, within the context of its work to promote all human rights.

SAVOLA GROUP
Our mission is to:
1. Manage and grow a portfolio of successful businesses with particular focus on Basic Foods.
2. Manage a balanced expansion program in Savola's chosen areas of activities in the Middle East, Asia, Africa, and elsewhere.
3. Grow into new sectors where Savola can leverage one or more of its core competencies and the strength of its balance sheet.

▶

DEVELOPING VISION AND MISSION STATEMENTS

COUNCIL OF AMERICAN ISLAMIC RELATIONS (CAIR)
To enhance understanding of Islam, encourage dialogue, protect civil liberties, empower American Muslims, and build coalitions that promote justice and mutual understanding.

ISLAMIC SOCIETY OF NORTH AMERICA
ISNA is an association of Muslim organizations and individuals that provides a common platform for presenting Islam, supporting Muslim communities, developing educational, social and outreach programs, and fostering good relations with other religious communities and civic and service organizations.

ISLAMIC MEDICAL ASSOCIATION OF NORTH AMERICA
To provide a forum and resource for Muslim physicians and other health care professionals, to promote a greater awareness of Islamic medical ethics and values among Muslims and the community-at-large, to provide humanitarian and medical relief, and to be an advocate in health care policy.

INDIAN MUSLIM RELIEF CHARITIES
To help India's Muslims achieve security, freedom, and equality – their rights as citizens of India.

AMERICAN RED CROSS
To improve the quality of human life; to enhance self-reliance and concern for others; and to help people avoid, prepare for, and cope with emergencies.

ONTARIO FEDERATION OF TEACHING PARENTS
We envision universal acknowledgement and acceptance of home-based education as a viable educational model. OFTP will be recognized as a significant and valuable authority and advocate for home-based education in Ontario.

MUSLIM COMMUNITY ASSOCIATION OF THE SAN FRANCISCO BAY AREA (MCA)
We are the Muslim Community Association of the San Francisco Bay Area. In cooperation with Muslim communities

4
DEVELOPING VISION AND MISSION STATEMENTS

around the Bay Area, our mission is to live our faith as a congregation, inspired by the teachings of the Qur'an and Prophet Muhammad as individuals and as a collective body, and to foster a mission of peace, justice and compassion for all within our Mosque, our community and the world.

ISLAMIC CENTER OF LONG ISLAND
To serve and engage Muslims by promoting the progressive values and teachings of Islam, and to advocate interfaith harmony in a multicultural environment in accordance with the Qur'an and Sunnah.

EDHI FOUNDATION (PAKISTAN)
The mission of the Edhi Foundation is to motivate the people in Pakistan and other third world countries to resolve their social and other problems on (a) self-help basis. Edhi emphasizes the importance of safeguarding the basic human rights, regardless of religion, caste, or creed.

McDONALDS
To offer the fast-food customer food prepared in the same high-quality manner world-wide, tasty and reasonably priced, delivered in a consistent, low-key decor and friendly atmosphere.

Linking Vision and Mission to Values

The organization's mission statement frequently reflects its values. Values, which describe the beliefs and principles built into the organization's way of doing things, encapsulate what participants feel strongly about. For example, the McDonalds' mission statement (see illustration capsule 3 (a)) highlights this firm's emphasis on quality, consistency, and friendliness. Similarly, the Edhi Foundation's mission statement emphasizes self-help, while that of the MCA highlights peace, justice, and compassion. A statement of philosophy or values is often provided to guide the organization's pursuit of its vision and mission. It usually contains four to eight values and reinforces the organization's overall direction. Examples of various organizations' statements of philosophy or values are included in illustration capsule 3 (b).

> A Muslim organization's mission statement often reflects the values built into the organization's way of doing things.

Defining a Statement of Philosophy or Values

A statement of philosophy or values details the fundamental principles and values that underlie everything the organization or corporation does. This philosophy enunciates the manner in which either the Islamic organization or corporation serves its mission and its customers.

When drafting a statement of philosophy, use worksheet #10 (Appendix A, p. 173). In general, seek to answer the following two questions:

- How will our organization members or corporate employees conduct themselves while carrying out our mission?
- What are the values of our organization or business?

It is important that the statement of philosophy or values be included in your organization's or corporation's official documents (e.g., annual reports and personnel manual). Do not make it too complex or too long – a couple of paragraphs is enough. A statement of philosophy for a hypothetical Islamic organization concerned about environmental issues could read as follows:

> *The Islamic Environmental Conservancy will act in accordance with the highest standards of ethics, as defined by the Shari`ah, accountability, and transparency. We affirm that the environment is an amanah (trust) given to humanity, and to the Muslim community in particular, by Allah. Hence, it is a divine trust. We view our responsibility with a deep sense of commitment and respect, and will use a balanced, fair, and open approach in our advocacy.*

Illustration capsule 3 (b) contains statements of philosophy or values from several organizations.

Illustration Capsule 3 (b)
Examples of Statements of Philosophy

AMNESTY INTERNATIONAL
Amnesty International is independent of any government, political ideology, economic interest, or religion. It does not support or oppose any government or political system, nor does it support or oppose the views of the victims whose rights it seeks to protect. It is concerned solely with the impartial protection of human rights.

4 DEVELOPING VISION AND MISSION STATEMENTS

SAVOLA GROUP
- We intend well.
- We work on making these intentions sincere.
- We believe Allah's Blessings will be there supporting those who maintain good and sincere intentions.

COUNCIL ON AMERICAN ISLAMIC RELATIONS
- CAIR supports free enterprise, freedom of religion and freedom of expression.
- CAIR is committed to protecting the civil rights of all Americans, regardless of faith.
- CAIR supports domestic policies that promote civil rights, diversity and freedom of religion.
- CAIR opposes domestic policies that limit civil rights, permit racial, ethnic or religious profiling, infringe on due process, or that prevent Muslims and others from participating fully in American civic life.
- CAIR is a natural ally of groups, religious or secular, that advocate justice and human rights in America and around the world.
- CAIR supports foreign policies that help create free and equitable trade, encourage human rights and promote representative government based on socio-economic justice.
- CAIR believes the active practice of Islam strengthens the social and religious fabric of our nation.
- CAIR condemns all acts of violence against civilians by any individual, group or state.
- CAIR advocates dialogue between faith communities both in America and worldwide.
- CAIR supports equal and complementary rights and responsibilities for men and women.

MUSLIM COMMUNITY ASSOCIATION OF SAN FRANCISCO BAY AREA

In pursuit of our mission, we choose to emphasize these particular values:
- The goodness and the love of God manifested in all creation.
- The dignity of the person called to wholeness by God.
- The spiritual power of community committed to prayer and service.

Mission Statements of the Organization's Subunits

After the SPC has helped your organization develop its mission statement, it should help functional (e.g., marketing, finance) or product/service (e.g., *halal* meat production, bookstore, conference) managers develop mission statements focused on functional- or product-level activities. Other organizations usually entrust this responsibility to the department head or the committee chair. Generally, the mission statement's level of specificity increases the further down you go in an organization. However, one common element remains whether you are running a not-for-profit organization or a business: The organization's mission statement subsumes the mission statements of all its subunits. Hence, they need to reflect the same core values and the same strategic intent enunciated at the organization level.

Functional area mission statements emphasize the department's contribution to the organization's vision and mission, its role within the organization, and what it intends to do.[24] An example of a mission statement for a training and development department would be to enhance organizational effectiveness by developing future leaders and establishing a culture of trust and self-reliance.

CHAPTER 5

IDENTIFYING AND PRIORITIZING GOALS

Goals list the long-term, strategic priorities of the organization, and should be implemented in order of priority.

Whenever Allah's Apostle was given the choice of one of two matters, he would choose the easier of the two, as long as it was not sinful to do so, but if it was sinful to do so, he would not approach it.

(Narrated by Aisha[1])

Once the SPC has crafted your organization's vision and mission statement, it needs to return to the SWOT analysis to identify those goals or strategic priorities that will add the most value. In general, goals:

1. List the priority areas on which the organization wishes to focus its attention and resources,
2. Are long-term oriented, and
3. Should be implemented in order of priority.

Outlining Goals

For outlining goals, use worksheet #11 (Appendix A, p. 174). A basic rule is that the SPC should attempt to match the most attractive open opportunity to the most powerful strength or competency controlled by the organization. However, as pointed out earlier, an organization cannot always take advantage of the most promising opportunity[2] if it lacks the competency or internal discipline necessary to pursue it.

5
IDENTIFYING AND PRIORITIZING GOALS

Another problem that may arise during the goal selection process is that emotions may hijack the choice and ranking of strategic priorities. Organizations are *boundedly rational*,[3] and therefore are likely to choose the first goals that meet minimum criteria and upon which everyone can agree. In contrast, Thomas Edison, the inventor of the electric light bulb, initially came up with several dozen filaments for his bulb. He proceeded to test them to find out which one, given certain criteria, would work the best. But he did not stop at the first filament that worked; rather, he selected the one that best met his criteria. Similarly, stopping at the first agreed-upon goal may be dysfunctional if additional potential goals are not searched for and examined within the time allocated for this stage of strategy formulation. In a worst-case scenario, the SPC may succumb to groupthink and give credence to only those goals proposed by the leader or a very charismatic SPC member.

One of the better ways to resolve such a distortion is to gauge the relative impact of implementing each goal and then choose a selective set of goals based on the Pareto Rule. Briefly stated, the Pareto Rule states that 20 percent of the causes are responsible for 80 percent of the effects associated with any problem. Hence, choosing and implementing the top four goals from a potential set of 20 may achieve 80 percent of the organization's strategic plan.

To help select the top four goals in a relatively conflict-free manner, you could ask the SPC to use the green dot balloting process mentioned in chapter 3. Have each participant announce his/her top two goals and then go around the room until you have written down on an easel pad a list of unique, non-duplicated goals (each goal being identified by a letter, as shown in exhibit A). Next, distribute a fixed number of green dots to each participant using the 1/5 ratio (i.e., if there are 20 goals listed, give each participant 4 dots). Ask them to allocate the dots among the goals and write the letter(s) associated with the "most important" goal on the dot. Thus, if goal E is considered most important, it may receive 3 dots; if goal A is considered the next most important, it may receive 1 dot; and the other goals would receive no dots at all. Ask participants to stick their green dot(s) on the easel pad next to the goals they chose. The resulting ballot should look similar to exhibit A, and a quick visual count should tell you the goals' order of priority.

> According to the Pareto Rule, addressing 20 percent of the causes may take care of 80 percent of the effects associated with any problem.

Illustration Capsule 4

Examples of Goals

IMRC's Goals
- To provide health care to Indians in general, and to Indian Muslims in particular.

Ameen Housing Co-op
- Foster Islamic investment practices which benefit economic, religious and social aspects of a member's life and the Muslim community at-large.
- Help members purchase homes with an interest-free alternative to the society's demands.
- Assist in establishing Muslim Communities across North America.

Muslim Community Association of San Francisco Bay Area
- To live and share our faith with all of God's people.
- To teach Islamic beliefs and values in the context of deepening spirituality and community involvement.
- To inspire leaders for stewardship in community service.
- To make our Mosques vital centers for worship and community needs.
- To empower the community to lead an Islamic way of life.

CHAPTER 6

GAP ANALYSIS

يَٰٓأَيُّهَا ٱلَّذِينَ ءَامَنُوٓاْ أَوْفُواْ بِٱلْعُقُودِ

O you who believe! Fulfill (all) obligations. (Qur'an, 5:1)

After performing the SWOT analysis, the SPC must assess any gap between the Islamic organization's current performance and the performance required for implementing its vision, mission, and goals. If your organization is strategy savvy and has a strategic plan that it has already started to implement, you may wish to look at chapter 14, where we discuss in detail how to conduct a performance assessment. Ideally, these measures should have been developed concurrently with your strategic and operational or action plans, and should have been monitored during strategy implementation. If such was the case, measuring any departures from the performance measures and precisely gauging the gap between your intended and your actual strategy should be quite easy.

Once these gaps are pinpointed, the SPC must develop explicit bridging strategies. If there is no gap, it may mean that your organization should be performing at a higher level. If the gap cannot be bridged in spite of your best efforts, the SPC must adjust the strategic plan to make

6
GAP ANALYSIS

it more realistic and achievable. It is better to prune those parts of the plan that have unbridgeable gaps than to let them linger on for years and create false expectations. Your plan should outline what you and your organization can realistically expect to deliver. This is how you build credibility and trust with respect to your core constituencies and external stakeholders.

Closing the Performance Gap

The SPC can be quite creative in finding ways to close the gap. Under conditions of rapid growth, the SPC may recommend an entrepreneurial turnaround strategy focusing on innovative products and services. Conversely, when the environment is stagnant, a retrenchment turnaround strategy may be followed to selectively prune unnecessary ancillary activities in order to sharpen the organization's focus. If your organization cannot achieve certain goals by itself, perhaps it should form a strategic alliance or a joint merger with other Islamic organizations. During the height of the Serbs' genocidal campaign against Muslim Bosnians, leading Islamic organizations in North America realized that they could not muster any efficient international support for the victims unless they built a strategic alliance. Therefore, a Bosnian Task Force was formed to bring together the major Islamic organizations. With Allah's help and the assistance of other faith-based communities, the task force achieved its goal of helping the Bosnian Muslims.

> Should your organization be unable to close a gap after reformulating its goals, consider dropping or postponing some of them— as the Prophet Muhammad did at Hudaybiyyah.

Should your organization be unable to close a gap even after reformulating its goals, consider dropping some of them. Events and circumstances sometimes require postponing a goal's implementation. While this may be a bitter pill for some members of your Islamic organization to swallow, they only need to remember what happened at Hudaybiyyah: The Muslims had to abandon their hajj, much against their will. However, this turned out to be only a temporary setback in Islam's march across Arabia.

CHAPTER 7

CRAFTING STRATEGIES

Strategies should stem from *profound understanding* rather than *emotional bravado*.

A strategy is the pattern or plan that integrates an organization's major goals, policies, and action sequences into a cohesive whole. A well-formulated strategy helps to marshal and allocate an organization's resources into a unique and viable posture based upon its relative internal competencies and shortcomings, anticipated changes in the environment, and contingent moves by intelligent opponents.

(James Brian Quinn[1])

When developing strategies, leaders of Islamic organizations need to revisit their SWOT analysis and focus on their organization's core competencies. Many strategic thinkers recommend that you base your strategies on *understanding* rather than *bravado*.[2] Thus, if an Islamic business has a group of well-trained, highly qualified software programmers, it would not make sense for them to go into the perfume or prayer-cap business.

In designing strategies, then, a basic principle is to challenge your opponents on your own terms, not theirs. As indicated by Khan, we can derive this principle from the events surrounding the treaty of Hudaybiyyah.[3] Since the unbelievers found themselves in an advantageous position, they naturally wanted to fight the Muslims. Inspired by

7
CRAFTING STRATEGIES

Allah, the Prophet understood the strategic importance of restraint and accepted their conditions, even though it disturbed many of his Companions. However, the resulting ten-year peace treaty changed the field of activity from the battlefield to the field of ideology and ideas. Within two years, Islam emerged victorious because of its ideological clarity and superiority.

Important Strategy Dimensions

Other dimensions of strategy[4] that Muslims need to pay attention to are:

- **Forward-looking:** Given that your strategy outlines a series of action sequences, it must be forward-looking and based on the SPC's understanding and forecasts about your organization's environment.

- **Proactive:** Since the external environment is dynamic and anticipatory, your strategy needs to consider your competitors' reaction to your organization's initiatives so that you can prepare an effective response.

- **Dynamic**: The external environment's dynamic nature and potential competitors' moves and countermoves mean that leaders of Islamic organizations must be quick on their feet and ready to act at any time.

- **Value-driven**: When choosing goals and strategies, managers should attempt to maximize the firm's total value and select value-driven goals by correlating organizational abilities with market opportunities to maximize the firm's value. Your organization may not necessarily pursue the most promising opportunity due to an inability to harness it. At the same time, however, the organization may not be using its top core competencies if nobody wants the products or services that these competencies produce. For example, your company may be the best in the world at producing typewriters, but clearly the world no longer uses them. Hence, it would be unwise for your company to produce obsolete products or provide unnecessary services

- **Adaptive**: Very often, an organization will list the strategies that it intends to adopt for different goals. These strategies may be similar to what worked in the past. However, because of the environment's dynamic nature, it is likely that what worked in the past may now be obsolete or even inappropriate. As a result, companies may find out that the set of strategies that they actually use (realized strategies) are quite different from those that they initially intended to use. These realized strategies are adaptive, given that they emerged from a changing situational context. As long as the strategies are not unethical, the outcomes sought are what matter.

What Strategy Involves

In general, your organization's strategy answers the question "how?":

- How to satisfy your stakeholders (e.g., customers, regulators, donors, or investors).
- How to grow the organization to better serve your customers.

Worksheet #12 (Appendix A, p. 175) will help you draft your organization's strategies. In designing strategies for any Islamic organization (e.g., a mosque, a shopping mall, a computer store, or a religious foundation [*waqf*]), your answers to the above questions reveal what you need to do.

1. ***Prioritize goals***
   In general, goals should be implemented according to their priority. Note that priorities can change in a turbulent environment and that you must then reorder your organization's goals. Each goal must be tied to your organization's strategies. In addition, each goal may have several strategies. It is very rare for one strategy to bring about the implementation of one goal, for each goal may have several parts that need to be addressed by a strategy tailored just for one particular part.

2. ***Develop a sustainable competitive advantage or position***
   Islamic organizations must compete, all the while remaining within the bounds of Islamic ethics. Islam, in fact, encourages market competition. For instance, Saeed et al. cite the following incident [5]: Once Umar al-Khattab passed by Hatib ibn Abi Balta'ah and learned that he was selling raisins at a much lower price in order to ruin his competitors. Umar told him: "Either raise your rate or leave our market." From this and similar hadiths,[6] we can tell that Islam abhors price manipulation and encourages a free-market system and fair competition (*munafasah*). Islamic organizations should develop strategies to enhance their competitiveness and not restrict free-market competition.

7
CRAFTING STRATEGIES

3. ***Defend against threats to the organization***

    In a changing environment, Islamic organizations may find that other organizations meet their customers' needs more effectively. Strategies may be developed to enhance the quality of one's product or service, including building strategic alliances with other stakeholders. If your organization consistently performs poorly, perhaps you should retrench. As an Islamic not-for-profit organization, the money donated to your programs is an *amanah* (trust). If you cannot use these donations to serve Islam and Muslims with your current product or service offering, find another niche where you can be more effective. One national Islamic organization decided to sell its bookstore business after decades of poor performance when it realized that other competitors repeatedly outperformed it and that subsidizing continuous financial losses was no longer an option. The same is true for a business. If you are continuously losing money, find a niche that is still *halal* but is more aligned with your competencies. For example, Japan was outperforming Intel in memory chips. This eventually caused Intel to abandon that niche and become a microprocessor designer and manufacturer. Today, a majority of the world's desktops and notebooks run on Intel microprocessors, such as the Pentium chip.

4. ***Execute complementary and consistent strategies***

    As indicated earlier, strategy is both a single-action sequence and the unifying pattern underlying all of the different strategies. *Complementariness* means that the strategy used in one part of the organization should not hamper the strategy used in another part. *Consistency* means that although the organization may be using a defensive and then an offensive strategy, both strategies can help it succeed and achieve a sustainable competitive advantage. For example, a firm may be retrenching with respect to one market, but simultaneously expanding in another. The hijrah could be considered the Prophet's retrenchment strategy; yet he was simultaneously expanding into Yathrib (pre-Islamic Madinah), where his message was more welcome. These two strategies differ, but when they are looked at within the context of his overall mission, they worked.

    Similarly, when Emperor Constantine stymied Sultan Fateh's navy by ordering a heavy chain laid across the Bosphorus and

CRAFTING STRATEGIES

making it impossible to block the Venetian ships resupplying enemy forces, the sultan ordered his boats to be withdrawn and towed, overnight, over a mountain and then relaunched from a place where they could go on the offensive. These dual strategies of retreat and offense were mutually complementary and consistent and, by Allah's Grace, led to the ultimate liberation of Constantinople. Internal consistency among the various strategies being employed to meet the organization's different goals is critical.

Figure 4 illustrates the interplay among multiple strategic moves for an Islamic organization. This hypothetical organization simultaneously uses defensive as well as offensive strategies. In response to the competitors' efforts to duplicate its products, the organization may drop its prices or narrow its product mix. At the same time, new customer needs may be surfacing. Hence, the organization may be developing new products or expanding its geographical domain. While each of these strategic moves is a strategy unto itself, the overall pattern of any strategic move also represents an organizational or a corporate strategy. An Islamic for-profit or not-for-profit organization can do both simultaneously, as long as one set of strategies does not stand in the way of a different set of strategies.

Figure 4
Organization Strategy as a Pattern of Actions

7
CRAFTING STRATEGIES

> Repeating the same strategy handed down by previous leaders or mindlessly copied from competitors may lead the organization into a rut.

5. **Be creative and do not repeat past mistakes**

    Organizations often get into a rut and need to re-assess what strategy is the most effective for achieving their mission and goals. Repeating the same strategy handed down by previous leaders or copied *ad nauseam* from competitors may lead nowhere. Just as Prophet Muhammad was willing to listen to Salman al-Farsi's innovative suggestion at Khandaq, contemporary Muslim leaders need to develop creative strategies within Islam's parameters. One such example comes from Pakistan's Edhi Foundation, an organization dedicated to helping the poor and the destitute to help themselves. This foundation has provided some unconventional welfare services, despite severe social and cultural opposition. For example, *jhoolas* (cradles) represent a creative solution to a very sad problem: Baby cradles are installed near most emergency Edhi centers, where unwanted children can be abandoned anonymously. Although some external stakeholders assert that this service encourages illegitimate childbirth, the foundation believes that these cradles prevent the even greater crime of abandoning unwanted babies to die in garbage dumps.

6. **Monitor strategy inflection points and respond to changing environmental conditions**

> When a previously effective strategy no longer works, a strategy *inflection point* may have been reached.

    An important skill that your Islamic organization may wish to develop is the ability to track strategy inflection points. As indicated by Intel's former CEO Andrew Grove, organizations should monitor the effectiveness of the strategies being used: "A key warning sign ... [of] ... a strategic inflection point is when all of a sudden, the company you worry about has shifted. You dealt with one competitor all your life, and all of a sudden you do not care about them, you care about somebody else. A mental silver bullet test ... [is] ... if you had one bullet, whom would you shoot with it? If you change the direction of the gun, that ... signals you may be dealing with more than an ordinary shift in the competitive landscape."[7] When the strategies begin to – and continue to – lose their effectiveness, as indicated by former peak performance levels never being reached and even declining despite your best efforts, a strategy inflection point has been reached. You should act immediately, and the organization should immediately try to adjust its strategy to fit the new circumstances.

CRAFTING STRATEGIES

Levels of Strategy

Strategy occurs at multiple levels. In a large Islamic corporation or organization, strategy occurs at five levels:

- **Enterprise.** Generally, the strategy here focuses on the general societal need being met.
- **Corporate.** Strategies here encompass the whole organization and its divisions or strategic business units (e.g., a charitable foundation, bookstore, or *da`wah*).
- **Business.** This type of strategy is a function of the company's degree of diversification. If this company has multiple divisions, then each business (division) should have its own strategy.
- **Functional.** Within each business unit (division), functional areas exist (e.g., accounting, marketing, sales, production, and research and development). Each functional area must tackle the issue of strategy within each function.
- **Operating.** Key activities within each functional area need to have their own strategy (e.g., managing the fleet of cars or maintaining and/or upgrading the website).

For most small Islamic organizations, only the bottom three levels apply: organizational (corporate), functional (departments, committees, or task forces) and operating strategies. Figure 5 depicts this relationship:

Figure 5
Levels of Strategy for an Islamic Organization

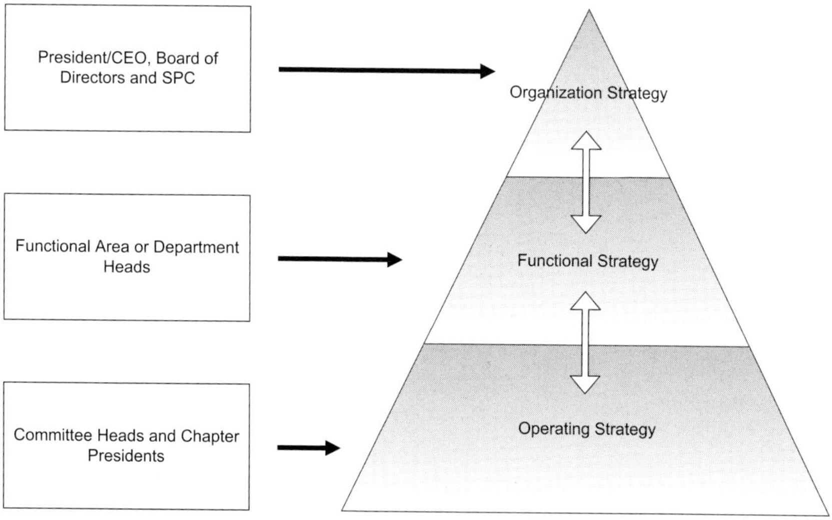

President/CEO, Board of Directors and SPC → Organization Strategy

Functional Area or Department Heads → Functional Strategy

Committee Heads and Chapter Presidents → Operating Strategy

7
CRAFTING STRATEGIES

Each level of strategy should be consistent with the higher and lower levels, for each level builds upon the one above it.

Illustration capsule 5 gives some examples of organization strategy.

Illustration Capsule 5
Examples of organization strategies

IMRC
- Educate people about health and healthcare.
- Emphasize preventive medicine.

McDonalds
- Add new restaurants annually or market expansion.
- Use new menu items and low-price specials to promote frequent customer visits.
- Choose sites convenient to customers.
- Focus on limited product line and consistent quality.

National Highway Traffic Safety Administration Strategies
- Set and enforce safety performance standards for motor vehicles.
- Promote safe driving behavior.

Four Tests of a Strategy's Effectiveness

How do you know whether your strategy is a winner? Thompson, Gamble, and Strickland propose three tests for determining this.[8] I have added a fourth one: ethics (*akhlaq*).

An Islamic organization should aim for adaptability rather than adaptation.

1. **The Goodness-of-Fit Test**

    How well does your Islamic organization's strategy fit its situation? Although you would want a tighter fit between your strategy and its external environment, it may be problematic. A tighter fit is not always better because of the distinction between *adaptation* and *adaptability*, for both are ways to adjust to the external environment's changing demands. However, they have distinctly different results. When an Islamic company engages in adaptation, it fits its customers' needs better than any other competitor in the short-term. However, any future change in the customers' needs will drive it out of business because it has so customized itself to fit the customers' current needs that it has become over-specialized and cannot adjust. In contrast, an Islamic company that engages in adaptability may meet its customers' current needs in a general manner, but also retain enough organizational slack (extra cushion of resources) to meet their future needs, should these change.

2. *The Competitive Advantage Test*

   Does strategy lead to competitive advantage? An Islamic business must not only develop a competitive advantage, but must also be able to maintain it (viz., achieve a sustainable competitive advantage). In this regard, systems theory talks of *dynamic equilibrium*, by which it means that an organization that is number one at one point in time may not continue its supremacy forever and may actually lose ground over time if it does not strive to maintain its competitive advantage. An excellent example is Turkey's Ottoman Bank. Once it was the central bank. However, its status declined because its leaders did not keep up with the changing times. Now, many competitors are thriving where it used to.

3. *The Performance Test*

   Does strategy boost organization performance? If the organization's strategy is not improving its performance (e.g., membership decreases, fundraising targets are missed, market share is being encroached upon, geographical coverage is shrinking), then decision makers need to rethink their organization's strategy. An excellent example is how Khalid ibn Walid adjusted the Muslims' army during the battle of Yarmuk after the first three days of battle: the numerically superior Byzantines almost managed to break through on a couple of fronts. So confident were they of success that some of them chained themselves to each other. Khalid realized early on that an offensive, frontal attack would surely be defeated, and so he combined defensive and offensive strategies, depending on what the Byzantines were doing.

7
CRAFTING STRATEGIES

> A Muslim organization that fails the *akhlaq* test has failed everything.

4. *The Ethics (Akhlaq) Test*

Your organization's strategy may have a proper fit with the external environment, may lead to sustainable competitive advantage, and may improve overall performance, but may still be wrong if it is unethical. Let us assume that you are a Muslim doing business in a country where unethical practices are the norm, where cheating allows you to run your competitors out of business and obtain high profits by gouging your customers. If you engage in these practices, have you behaved Islamically and ethically? As someone once said, if you win the rat race, you are still a rat! In chapter 16, the link between strategy and ethics will be covered in much greater detail.

CHAPTER 8

DEVELOPING MEASURABLE OBJECTIVES

Given the specificity of objectives, some leaders of Islamic organizations avoid them to dodge accountability, are reluctant to terminate old (and failed) projects, or engage in activities that are not directly tied to their mission (e.g., traveling, giving speeches, cultivating a rock star image). If you want to avoid organizational decline and decay, set and implement SMART objectives.

SMART Criteria

Objectives, the specific action steps that have to be taken to achieve goals, must meet SMART (viz., specific, measurable, acceptable, realistic, time-bound) criteria. They must be:

Objectives which meet SMART criteria will facilitate gap analysis and performance assessment.

- **Specific**: What (part of the goal) are you focusing on? Some goals may be immense, such as wishing to raise the ethical level of your nation's business community. But to achieve this desirable goal, you may need to break it into smaller, more manageable segments and attach a specific objective to each segment. As Kouzes and Posner indicate, the most effective leader is one who plans small wins.[1] This approach makes the goal and its associated objectives appear much less daunting, and earlier successful implementations of small objectives tend to have a multiplier, motivational effect.

8
DEVELOPING MEASURABLE OBJECTIVES

- **Measurable**: How much is to be achieved? Your organization's objectives must be quantitative, because this is how progress toward their achievement can be measured. Later, as your organization implements these measurable objectives, any gap between the intended and the realized target should be scrutinized. Do not leave the numbers attached to an objective vague or "something to be agreed upon at a later date," for this is no more than passing the buck. Being "nice" or diplomatic here can actually hurt your organization's long-term performance and its effort to serve Allah.

- **Acceptable**: Is the objective acceptable to those who will implement it? This criterion is critical, for no amount of sophisticated planning matters if the plan is not implemented. Unless the implementers wholeheartedly accept the plan as well as the objectives assigned to them, the plan is as good as dead from the start. The team leader entrusted with meeting an objective must be passionate about it and take ownership of it. The objective is now theirs; they will champion it and see it through. You will not have to goad or remind them.

- **Realistic**: What is the outcome? Is it challenging yet achievable? Your organization's objectives must be flexible, because this is how it will move from where it is now to where it ideally wants to be. At the same time, the objective must not be so difficult as to discourage its implementers. Do not set the bar too high or too low.

- **Time bound**: What is the deadline for meeting the objective? The implementers must have a clear idea of this date. Otherwise, they will get in each other's way and may even come into conflict with each other as key elements of the objectives or the necessary resources do not come online at the appropriate time.

> If current performance is not measured against the intended objective in a systematic manner, the motivation and accountability of those entrusted with implementation will be weak.

To reiterate, goals and objectives are not the same. Goals focus on long-term priorities, rarely have a specific time component attached to them, and are usually implemented in order of priority. In contrast, objectives are attached to a specific goal and entity (e.g., a division, department, functional area, committee) in order to maintain accountability. In addition, they are to be quantified as much as possible. The basic rule here is: *If it is not measured, it will not be accomplished.*

DEVELOPING MEASURABLE OBJECTIVES

Your vision statement is usually rather idealistic, but your objectives must be realistic. Tie your objectives to a budget based on a realistic income stream.

Illustration Capsule 6a
Examples of Organization Objectives

IMRC:
Goal: To provide health care to Indians in general, and to Indian Muslims in particular.

Strategies:
- To educate people about health and health care.
- To emphasize preventive medicine.

Objective:
- To establish 3 mobile clinics by end of 1992.

ISNA:
Goal: To produce well-rounded and capable Imams and leaders for the North American Muslim community.

Strategies:
- To offer various types and levels of training programs that combine knowledge of Islam and leadership skills.
- To identify and/or publish material relevant to the goal.
- To offer mentorship opportunities for Imams and leaders.
- To reactivate the Islamic Teaching Center to create an Imam and Leadership Training Center (ILTC).

Objective:
- To establish the Center by hiring a director and executive assistant before the end of 2003.

The EDHI Foundation:
Objectives:
- The establishment / extension of additional Edhi homes for the destitute during the next three years is planned for all major cities. These cities include Peshawar, Quetta,

8
DEVELOPING MEASURABLE OBJECTIVES

> Muzaffarabad, Chitral, Gujranwala, and Lahore. The estimated cost of the above facilities is over Rs. 100 million.
> - The number of ambulances will be increased from an existing 400 ambulances to 650 ambulances over the next two years. The total cost of ambulance centers and associated ambulances will be approximately Rs. 56 million.
> - In order to run EDHI services and meet recurrent expenditures on long-term footing, the foundation hopes to raise Rs. 400 million within the next 5 years as a reserve fund which will act as a fixed deposit base.

When SMART objectives are defined appropriately, your Islamic organization can easily evaluate its own performance (see chapter 10). The strategic plan's objectives establish benchmarks to gauge whether the organization is on track or drifting away. Given the dynamic nature of an Islamic organization's work, its objectives should be revisited periodically to make sure that they fit in with the remainder of the strategic plan and are eliciting the intended level of performance. Doing this once or twice a year is sufficient, unless the external environment is turbulent. As Migliore et al. indicate, objectives also represent a performance contract between the leader and his/her followers and should be written down accordingly.[2]

Examples of Poor vs. Good Objectives

Writing your objectives down makes it easy to spot those that are poorly expressed or do not meet SMART criteria. Consider these objectives:

Illustration Capsule 6b
How To Write a Good Objective

Example 1	
Poor objective:	To maximize membership within two years.
Issues:	What does "maximize" mean? Are we going to open our doors to anyone who knocks on them? Are there any filters that should be applied to potential members (e.g., level of education, area of specialization)?

DEVELOPING MEASURABLE OBJECTIVES

Improved Objective:	Our objective is to increase membership among professional sisters by 10% each year for the next 5 years.
Example 2	
Poor Objective:	To maximize the sales revenue and profit of our Islamic books.
Issues:	One cannot maximize sales revenue and profits at the same time. If I want to maximize profits, I could sell each book at a high price. This would maximize the profit per book, but the total sales revenue would decrease as a result.
Improved Objective:	Our objective is to increase sales revenue by 50% and profits by 10% by the end of next year.
Example 3	
Poor Objective:	To become the most effective Islamic organization.
Issues:	In which geographical area? "Effective" according to whose criteria? Different stakeholders use different criteria to assess organizational effectiveness, and very often the criteria used by different parties contradict each other.
Improved Objective:	Our objective is to become the leading *da`wah*-oriented organization for Muslim converts in the U.K. and Ireland by 2007.

CHAPTER 9

DEVELOPING OPERATIONAL PLANS

A strategic plan must be translated into an operational plan to facilitate short-term implementation.

Shura is critical in helping a leader during both strategy formulation and implementation.

Effective strategic plan implementation depends on people. Picking the right person for implementation is absolutely critical, as indicated by Khalid ibn al Walid, the best strategist in Islamic history. At the onset of the battle of Yarmuk, where the Muslims faced a far more numerous Byzantine army, Abu Ubaydah, the general appointed by Umar to lead the Muslim army, delegated this task to Khalid. Khalid agreed: "*Abu Ubaydah is a man of the purest character, but he does not know the stratagems of war.*"[1] Realizing that he was, by the grace of the Almighty, the right person to lead the army, this seasoned veteran went on to win another major victory.

Commenting on the importance of selecting the right person, Beekun and Badawi indicate that it may not always be possible to find a strong Muslim with the requisite skills.[2] In fact, an Islamic organization may have to choose between a strong Muslim with weak leadership skills and a strong leader with moderate or weak Islamic understanding. Amr ibn al-'As had only been a Muslim for four months when the Prophet appointed him to lead the Muslims at the battle of Dhat al-Salasil. Ibn Taymiyyah provides a rationale for this decision in his *As-Siyasah al-Shar`iyyah*.[3] A leader with weak or inadequate expertise can bring disaster to an organization, whereas a skilled leader may advance and help it. Even if a skilled leader is not a strong Muslim, his shortcomings can be made up through the *shura* process of decision-making, sound advice (*nasihah*), and the implementation of jointly agreed-upon goals.

9
DEVELOPING OPERATIONAL PLANS

Operational Plans

After formulating the organization's strategic plan, the SPC should turn its attention to shorter-term plans, namely, *operational* or *tactical* plans, for each key results area.[4] The plans developed for each of these areas typically cover a span of one year. Strategic and operational planning are rarely done at the same time and by the same people. An operational plan needs to focus on the following:

1. In order to offer products or services consistent with our strategic plan, what are our short-term objectives (targets) within the next year? Targets are SMART, shorter-term actions designed to accomplish longer-term objectives. Each target may be subdivided into sequential activities, must have a time component (usually a year or less), and should always be attached to specific units (e.g., functional areas, departments, or committees). To repeat, the length of time attached to a target may be less than one year, depending on the velocity of the external environment. A faster, more turbulent environment makes it harder to forecast far into the future and requires much shorter time frames with respect to targets.

2. Which performance measures can we use to gauge our progress toward meeting these targets?

3. How will we reach these short-term objectives? In other words, what human, financial, and other resources can we assign to each objective? Resources are the means by which we can accomplish predetermined activities, including plant, labor, raw material, and other assets.

Functional, Departmental, or Committee Plans

After developing the organization's strategic and operational plans, it is time to develop functional area plans (e.g., finance, human resources, operations), departmental, and/or committee plans. These must be communicated and agreed upon so that they will be carefully aligned with the organizational level plans (strategic and operational). Again, this is an iterative, not a top-down, process that requires both lateral and vertical communication as well as coordination across product and service areas and/or functional areas.

Both lateral and vertical (downward and upward) communication are critical in the iterative process of developing and implementing operational plans.

To ensure that the various levels of the organization's plans work together in a coordinated manner, the SPC and you, as the leader or the CEO, must stay vigilant and keep a bird's eye view of the whole planning landscape. While you should rarely get involved in operational details, you may delegate key tasks without abdicating your own responsibility. Throughout the implementation process, use your own leadership skills, an appropriate organizational structure, and a culture based on excellence to execute the strategic and operating plans. At all times, stay focused on the organization's shared vision. It is your responsibility, and nobody else's, to be the drumbeater and cheerleader who galvanizes your followers into action.

An example of an operational plan from IMRC and SMO (a hypothetical composite Muslim student organization based on several existing organizations) is given in illustration capsule 7.

Illustration Capsule 7
Example of an Operational Plan

IMRC:
GOAL (1990): To provide health care to Indians in general, and to Indian Muslims in particular.
STRATEGIES:
- To educate people about health and health care.
- To emphasize preventive medicine.

LONG-TERM OBJECTIVE: To establish 3 mobile clinics by end of 1992.

SHORT-TERM OBJECTIVES OR TARGETS: (linked to 1-year, short-term objectives):
- Survey needy areas by mid-1991 (task assigned to A,M)
- Purchase equipment by end-1991 (task assigned to M,J)
- Staff the clinic by March 1992 (task assigned to S,R)

RESOURCES:
- Volunteers from local organization (names listed).
- Unemployed medical doctors (names listed).

PERFORMANCE MEASURES:
- By January 1993, establishment of mobile clinics in needy areas in Bombay and Madras.
- By January 1995, decrease in pre-birth mortality rate in targeted areas.

9
DEVELOPING OPERATIONAL PLANS

> **SMO**
> **GOAL:**
> Increase SMO presence on North American campuses
> **STRATEGIES:**
> - Attract and retain more members
> - Educate members in *da`wah*
>
> **LONG-TERM OBJECTIVE:**
> To increase the number of registered SMO members to 10,000 within the next five years.
>
> **SHORT-TERM OBJECTIVE:**
> Decrease membership application processing time by 50% within 1 year.
>
> **ACTIVITIES:**
> - Streamline application form (assigned to specific individual)
> - Change membership database software (assigned to specific committee)
> - Train staff in new database software (assigned to specific individuals)
> - Test and refine new process (assigned to specific committee)
>
> **RESOURCES:**
> - Membership services staff (names listed)
> - Benchmarking organization (name listed)
> - Database software designer training staff (names listed)
>
> **PERFORMANCE MEASURES:**
> - 10% decrease in complaints from new applicants within 1 year.
> - All new membership applications to be processed within 3 days of receipt.

A more detailed example of SMO's operational plan with respect to the training activity is listed in illustration capsule 8. You can also use worksheet #13 (Appendix A, p. 176) to outline your operational plan. Your strategic plan must be translated into an operational plan for it to make sense to the implementers. Otherwise, it will remain too lofty and nebulous, and your followers or employees will find it difficult to translate the organizational plan into something meaningful and executable. It is possible that once they work on the operational plan, gaps between what is intended and what can be realistically accomplished will surface. If this happens, the strategic plan may have to be adjusted accordingly.

Illustration Capsule 8
Examples of an Operational Plan

Action Step, Task, or Activity	Responsible Person or Group	Begin Date	End Date	Estimated Hours	Cost
1. Evaluate various membership database software	Muhib to lead All play a role	4/20	4/21	8	$750
2. Select, purchase, and supervise the customization of database software	Nabeela and the information technology team	4/22	6/23	120	$6,000
3. Solution: Train 3 more staff members in the new database software	Nabeela/Issa	6/23	6/30	30	$1,000

Advice in Mapping Out Operational Plans

- Work for long-term goals while striving for small wins and immediate results. If you place too much emphasis on the long term, the day-to-day or month-to-month results may be neglected and end up suffering.
- When making short-term decisions, always keep your vision, mission, and goals in mind.

9
DEVELOPING OPERATIONAL PLANS

Delegate, but do not abdicate.

- Draw up clear targets, activities, and related directives. Make sure that all of these are clear to those who are expected to implement them. Post them on a large wall exhibit so that everyone can see at a glance what they are supposed to be working on and how much progress has been made.

- Do not assume that they understand. Use multiple channels of communication to make sure they do, such as face-to-face exchanges, group discussions, direct phone calls, e-mail, videos, and handouts. You may wish to store handouts and committee minutes on a secure intranet site so that implementers can retrieve them as needed.

- Keep the language of the operating plan simple and understandable.

- As indicated by Beekun and Badawi, delegate authority but do not abdicate responsibility.[5]

CHAPTER 10

DEVELOPING CONTINGENCY PLANS

Abu Hurayrah said: "The Prophet, peace be upon him, remarked: 'The example of a believer is like a fresh tender plant: From whichever direction the wind blows, it bends the plant. But when the wind dies down, it straightens up again. (Similarly a believer is tested by afflictions to strengthen his [her] faith and heart, and he [she] remains patient and firm.) And an evil person is like a pine tree that remains hard and stiff until Allah breaks it whenever He wills'." [1]

Uhud demonstrates the importance of contingency plans for Islamic organizations.

No strategic plan is ever perfect, and all of them are relatively rarely implemented as intended. The SPC must help the organization formulate possible alternative or contingency strategies in case events unfold in an unanticipated manner. An excellent example of changing a strategy occurred at the Battle of Uhud. Contrary to the Prophet's explicit directives, the Muslim archers abandoned their position on top of the hills at the rear and left the Muslim army exposed to Khalid ibn Walid's attack. Exhibit B depicts the Muslim archers' initial position, as dictated by the Prophet, their subsequent abandonment of these positions, and the brilliant countermove by Khalid, the only person to inflict a near-defeat on the Prophet.[2] If Allah wanted to test His Prophet and the Muslims with the bitter taste of Uhud, why should He spare you?

10
DEVELOPING CONTINGENCY PLANS

Just in case you encounter your own Uhud, develop contingency plans. Use a SWOT analysis to quickly develop and *rehearse* several contingency plans to deal with any emergent issues or problems. As we will discuss later, scenario building can really help you anticipate various types of change.

Developing a Process

As the SPC works through the strategic plan, its members need to anticipate the moves and countermoves of other sectors of the external and internal environments. Unless your Islamic organization wants to engage in management by activity and reaction (MAR), make every attempt to be proactive.

> Never have only one backup plan. Rehearse multiple contingency plans to deal with any emergent issues or problems.

Exhibit B: The Battle of Uhud

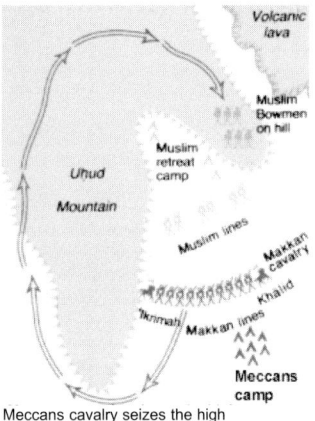

Meccans cavalry seizes the high ground once Muslims arrowmen left it for the plains.

[Reproduced from the online book *Khalid bin Al-waleed: The Sword of Allah* by A. I. Akram. http://www.swordofAllah.com, 1969.]

Constantly fighting fires can sap the life right out of your organization and its strategic plan by diverting your attention from your vision, mission, goals, and objectives.[3] A driving instructor once told me to "expect the unexpected." In other words, people and organizations will not always behave normatively but according to their own idiosyncrasies. To the extent that one understands and plans for some of these idiosyncrasies, road accidents can be mitigated. Similarly, a strategic plan that anticipates potential contingencies allows you the flexibility to deal with them on your own terms. God willing, you will not be totally taken by surprise.

DEVELOPING CONTINGENCY PLANS

> No such thing exists as a perfect strategic or operational plan.

Although it may never ascertain the whole range of possible contingencies, an effective SPC will indirectly devise a cognitive process for thinking proactively and responding to events that are not part of the formal strategic plan. Ultimately, this cognitive process may be one of the strategic management process' most desirable results, because it provides the leader and other key decision makers with a common cognitive template for dealing with unanticipated events.

The SPC must remember that there is no such thing as a perfect strategic or operational plan. As pointed out earlier, trying to create the perfect plan is a waste of scarce time and resources. Due to the environment's dynamic nature, a plan becomes increasingly obsolete as soon as it is formulated. Hence, contingency plans should always be formulated right along with your organization's strategic and operational plans.

Positive and Negative Contingencies

> Outline ahead of time the trigger points at which different contingency plans will kick in.

Most strategic planners try to anticipate problems but rarely think of how to make use of an opportunity that arises suddenly. A deep understanding of one's internal and external environments, acquired through a continuous SWOT process, will provide all of the information an organization needs to counter unexpected threats or take advantage of opportunities. Remember that although an opportunity may be extremely attractive, an organization should not rush into capturing it; there may simply be no fit between the opportunity and the current configuration of the organization's available resources. A good contingency template should filter out such tempting distractions.

In mapping out the organization's contingency plans, the SPC will also need to determine the trigger points at which these plans will kick in. For example, should revenues be unable to sustain expenses, the budget committee should be asked to recommend cutbacks or a retrenchment strategy. Alternately, the SPC may go one step further and recommend specific action sequences once a threshold point has been reached. Some threshold points may require tighter scrutiny instead of immediate action. Finally, the nature of the project being accomplished and the environment in which these projects exist can lower or raise thresholds. Thus, in a hyper-competitive environment where the rate of change is extremely fast and the degree and nature of change is itself unpredictable, thresholds could be raised and lead times for action could be shortened considerably in order to preempt the contingency plan's becoming obsolete. This is true for both opportunities and threats.

10
DEVELOPING CONTINGENCY PLANS

You should note here that Islam considers both positive and negative contingencies. The Qur'anic injunction to put in writing all contracts seeks to preempt future misunderstandings and problems. Similarly, *salat al-khawf* (the prayer of fear), discussed in *Sahih al-Bukhari* (hadith no. 6.59), allows Muslim soldiers to pray in groups while guarding against possible surprise attacks. Thus, contingency planning based on potential future scenarios is an inherent part of Islam.

Scenario Building

The motto of one of the major consulting outfits in scenario building is "Eyes on the Future, Feet on the Ground." This implies that while we cannot predict the future, since it is Allah's prerogative, we can attempt to anticipate the potential directions that the future course of events might take.

A scenario can be defined as "an internally consistent view of what the future might turn out to be – not a forecast, but one possible future outcome."[4] Thus, a scenario is a "storyline" that combines what we expect about the future with explorations of what may be possible.

> A scenario is 'an internally consistent view of what the future might turn out to be–not a forecast, but one possible future outcome.'

Scenario building has been practiced throughout Islamic history. Prophet Muhammad and Abu Bakr left Makkah for Madinah by the southern route, the exact opposite of what the enemy would expect. 'Amr ibn Fuhayrah, a shepherd, followed them with his flock in order to cover their tracks.[5] After the Ghassanids intercepted and executed the Prophet's envoy to the Governor of Bostra, Muhammad raised an army and put Zayd in charge. He told the soldiers to follow Ja`far if Zayd were killed and then 'Abdallah ibn Rawahah if Ja`far were killed. If all three were killed, then the Muslims should choose someone else to lead them.[6] In fact, this is exactly what happened at Mu'tah, where an alliance of the northern tribes and the imperial Byzantine troops vastly outnumbered the Muslims and killed these three leaders. Finally, Khalid was chosen as the new leader and then rallied the Muslims, checked the enemy's attacks, and led them in an orderly retreat.

Other examples of scenario building apply to one's daily life: performing *tayammum* (ablution with dust) if water is not available for *wudu'* (ablution), feeding poor people if you are sick and unable to fast, and eating pork – just enough to survive – if you are caught in a life-or-death situation with no other options.

Checklist for Building Scenarios

Schwartz describes the necessary steps for scenario building.[7] I summarize them here:

- **Identify focal issue or decision**

    For Islamic organizations in North America, the 9/11 terrorist attack was a major external environmental jolt, for such an event was totally unexpected. Muslims were shocked, saddened, and outraged. All of their strategic plans were thrown off course immediately, and the focal issue became clearing Islam's name and surviving as Muslims in North America. Many Muslim communities also dearly wanted to allay the ensuing alarm being experienced by our friends and neighbors of other faith-based communities

- **Pinpoint key forces in the local environment**

    Forces in the environment affect the outcome of decisions relating to the key issue(s) identified in step 1. These include legislative, political, religious, regulatory, and economic forces. Your organization's decision makers need to do their homework and determine what they need to know before making any decision. Obviously, acquiring accurate data is critical.

- **Determined driving forces in macro-environment**

    Driving forces are the major underlying causes of change.[8] Some of them stem from the macro-environment, while others originate from the organization's immediate local environment. Examples of driving forces are changes in information technology, laws (e.g., the Patriot Act and its potential variants), demography, government (who is or is not in power), public opinion, and lifestyle, as well as increases in uncertainty and business risk.

- **Rank by importance and uncertainty**

    Since some of the driving forces are more serious than others, they need to be ranked in terms of their importance to the pending decision and the level of uncertainty associated with them. Some predictable trends may actually rank higher than unpredictable ones. And, their ranking may change over time. For example, CAIR reports that the media's buffeting of Muslims and Islam in the post-9/11 environment is on the increase. A positive trend that initially counteracted this negative reaction was the tremendous wave of support and understanding shown by many

10 DEVELOPING CONTINGENCY PLANS

Americans and other faith-based communities. Recently, however, a CAIR public opinion survey of Americans revealed that the war in Iraq has taken its toll on the public's perception of Muslims and that hate crimes against Muslims have increased dramatically.

- **Select the scenario logics**

  Two or three driving forces can be used to create two-dimensional scenario maps. Several combinations of driving forces can be used to draw maps, one at a time. One driving force may be "governmental regulations" with its anchors ranging from "restrictive" to "open." Another driving force may be "media coverage" with its anchors ranging from "biased" to "balanced." Four potential scenarios could be developed:
  1. Restrictive/biased,
  2. Restrictive/balanced,
  3. Open/biased, and
  4. Open/balanced.

- **Flesh out the scenarios**

  Once the scenarios are set, a storyline can be developed for each by answering such questions as
  1. What events (international, national, local) need to occur for this scenario to emerge?
  2. What kind of actors (people) would enact these scenarios?
  3. What are the implications for your organization's strategy? This is the most important step. How does the issue to be decided upon fare under each of the possible scenarios? Is our strategy feasible under each possible scenario? Or else do we need to adjust our strategy for them to be workable under some of the scenarios?

- **Select leading indicators and signposts**

  What indicators and signposts do different parts of the organization need to recognize in order to locate it within the specific scenario being played out? Does the unit observing the indicator know how to act with respect to the indicator and its associated scenario(s)? What are the implications for your organization's strategy?

- Feed the scenarios back to those being consulted, and provide feedback to those being consulted about the issue or decision at hand.

> Select indicators and signposts so that decision-makers can locate the organization's role or part within the specific scenario being played out.

DEVELOPING CONTINGENCY PLANS

- **Discuss the strategic options**
  The decision-makers may then use *shura* to generate a strategy contingency grid (based partly on the scenario options matrix from Ringland[9]) and rate its elements from "very positive" to "very negative." Clearly, the options open to an organization will be a function of its core competencies. In a politically turbulent scenario, hiring extra legal staff, using public service announcements, and building strategic alliances would be positive, whereas the same options could be negative in a politically placid scenario.

Strategy Contingency Grid	Scenario 1	Scenario 2	Scenario 3
Strategy Alternative A	*	✔	X
Strategy Alternative B	*	X	X
Strategy Alternative C	✔	*	*
Strategy Alternative D	X	✔	*

* This strategy will work very well under this scenario.
✔ This strategy will work O.K. under this scenario.
X This strategy will not work under this scenario.

Watch out for diffusion of responsibility among team members; it may lead to everyone dodging assignments.

- **Agree on the implementation plan**
  When it has been decided to launch a specific project, appoint someone or a team as the project's owner and task him/her with the specific responsibility of tracking all relevant indicators, initiating early warning signals, establishing an agreed-upon contingency plan, and reporting back to the leader. Be careful when appointing a team as the project's owner/champion, for team processes may *diffuse* the *responsibility* among team members and enable everyone to pass the buck and dodge assignments.

- **Publicize the scenarios, if necessary**
  If circumstances require it, publicize some scenarios and their associated actions to sway the opinion of carefully selected target audiences. Be sure to choose these publicity channels carefully and assess the potential benefits/losses before doing so.

CHAPTER 11

IMPLEMENTING THE STRATEGIC PLAN: STRATEGY– LEADERSHIP FIT

فَإِنَّ مَعَ ٱلْعُسْرِ يُسْرًا ۝ إِنَّ مَعَ ٱلْعُسْرِ يُسْرًا ۝

So verily, with every difficulty there is relief. Verily, with every difficulty there is relief. (Qur'an, 94:5-6)

Execution – getting the task done, making it happen – is the most unappreciated skill of an effective (...) leader.
(Lou Gerstner, Jr., former CEO, IBM[1])

An effective leader is not only a visionary; he/she must also be able to execute.

Once the strategic, operational, and contingency plans are developed and agreed upon, implement them without delay. Every subsequent action undertaken by your members or employees should focus on whether or not their activities, either ongoing or planned, are moving the organization closer to its goals and objectives. If your strategy is to be implemented effectively, you must create a proper fit between your strategy and the three following elements:

- Your organization's capabilities, including leadership;
- Your organization's structure, including its internal support systems; and
- Your organization's culture and climate.

11
STRATEGY: LEADERSHIP FIT

I will discuss these macro-level variables in the next three chapters. Please note that the section on leadership and strategy implementation is discussed in much greater detail in *Leadership: An Islamic Perspective*.[2] Several leadership issues discussed there are omitted here, such as delegation, motivation, and the Islamic leadership paradigm. Part of the following section borrows from that book but has been considerably expanded.

A Five-Step Model of Leadership Effectiveness

Leadership can be defined as "a dynamic relationship based on mutual influence and common purpose between leaders and collaborators in which both are moved to higher levels of motivation and moral development as they affect real, intended change."[3] Burns defines leadership as "leaders inducing followers to act for certain goals that represent the values and the motivations – the wants and needs, the aspirations and expectations – of both *leaders and followers*."[4] Both definitions stress the *transformational* dimension of leadership whereby you, as the leader, and your followers enrich each other. Whereas *transactional* leaders approach followers with an eye to exchanging one thing for another (e.g., jobs for votes, board positions for donations), transformational leaders recognize the needs of potential followers and seek to fulfill their higher-order needs.[5] They strive to engage the follower's full person in order to engender mutual inspiration and elevation.

> Both transformational and transactional leaders are critical to organizations.

The transformational dimension is very much a part of the Islamic paradigm of leadership, which stresses the reciprocal enrichment of the leaders and the followers. In fact, Islam demands that you, as a leader, pay attention to your followers' needs. In a hadith (no. 2942) reported in *Sunan Abu Dawud* by Abu Maryam al-Azdi, the Prophet said:

> *If Allah puts anyone in the position of authority over the Muslims' affairs and he secludes himself (from them), not fulfilling their needs, wants, and poverty, Allah will keep Himself away from him, not fulfilling his need, want, and poverty.*[6]

At the same time, your followers must provide you with sincere and impartial feedback, support you, and help you orient yourself toward

> Umar said: 'May God have mercy upon anyone who points out my faults to me.'

> Learning from Prophet Muhammad, Umar became the quintessential Level 5 leader.

the good. Umar said: "May God have mercy upon anyone who points out my faults to me." In fact, your followers are responsible for following your directives as long as you behave Islamically, and for disobeying you when you do not. According to a hadith reported by *Sahih al-Bukhari* (no. 5.629) and narrated by Imam Ali, the Prophet said: "Obedience (to somebody) is required when he enjoins what is good."[7]

Although you may behave in accordance with Islamic precepts and enjoin the good, you might also become too engrossed in your duties as a leader and thus make yourself inaccessible. Leaders of Islamic organizations are sometimes perceived as aloof and/or unapproachable once they reach a certain level of success. Collins analyzes the leadership style of some of the world's best corporate leaders and uncovers a dimension that he calls level 5 leadership.[8] In contrast to those high-profile leaders who thrive on personality cults, Collins indicates that level 5 leaders are a paradoxical blend of personal humility and professional will (e.g., Umar and the personal humility he displayed while traveling to Jerusalem to receive its keys). The degree of humility and access suggested by level 5 leadership are critical to the effective implementation of an Islamic organization's strategy.

One of the best integrative models of effective leadership is inextricably connected with transformational leadership, level 5 leadership, and innovation.[9] This model consists of five basic practices that you, as a leader, can adopt. We will now discuss the leadership practices suggested by this model in the context of strategy implementation.

1. **Challenging the Process**

   Leadership is an active and dynamic process. The founders of the Muslim Students' Association of the USA and Canada were true pioneers at a time when Islam was just beginning to spread in America. Malcolm X, after discovering true Islam during his pilgrimage to Makkah, did not hesitate to do a complete turnaround: He started rethinking his previous beliefs based on black superiority and then began to proclaim the universal message of Islam. He paid dearly – with his life, in fact – for speaking and living the truth.

   While ineffectual leaders sit around and react to events, successful Muslim leaders seek Allah's help and challenge the status quo. In challenging the process, you have to be innovative. At times, you will need to redefine the process in a way that

11
STRATEGY: LEADERSHIP FIT

tears down the physical and mental barriers that others have imposed on the Muslim community. For example, dynamic Muslim leaders in India refuse to allow non-Muslims to label and classify Indian Muslims as "untouchables." When redefining the situation of Muslims, be careful not to overstep Islamic boundaries, as several people and groups have done recently.

While challenging the process, search for opportunities both inside and outside your organization or business. Look for ways to change or improve the status quo. These new opportunities may include an innovative new service or activity, reorganization, or a realignment of the organization's mission. To make this search fruitful, follow Allah's *shura* mandate, and consult with all manner of people, regardless of whether or not they belong to your organization. Even if you do not always agree with them, make it a point to listen to your most demanding critics. The most effective Islamic leaders that I work with use *shura* as part of their daily decision-making heuristics. Employing this process enables your followers to provide critical insights, since they are often the ones closest to the problem areas and know what does and does not work.

Experiment and take risks while challenging the process with the understanding that you may not always succeed. Each failure, however, can be viewed as a learning opportunity. For example, let's assume that you are learning how to play soccer. If you stand behind the ball but do not try to kick it, what have you learned? How can you improve your soccer skills? Similarly, if you have never opened your community's mosque up to members of other faith-based communities, how can you learn to work with them? You cannot shout for public help in times of need when you refuse to honor their request for your assistance. Go on; try, experiment, and fail if need be, but get up and improve.

While challenging the status quo, you, as a leader will often encounter many challenges. For example, you may be assailed by your fellow Muslims more viciously than by members of other faith-based communities. At times, your family may be harassed. You may even be asked to step down as president or CEO. You may pay dearly for seeking to make a positive difference, and may wonder why you are making such sacrifices when no one

> 'He who mixes with people and endures the harm they do is better than he who does not mix with them or endure the harm they do.'
> – Prophet Muhammad

appreciates them. Before giving up and accepting the status quo, remember the following hadith of the Prophet narrrated by Abdullah ibn Umar and reported by Al-Tirmidhi (hadith no. 5087) and Ibn Majah:

> *He who mixes with people and endures the harm they do is better than he who does not mix with them or endure the harm they do.*[10]

You may also wish to reflect on the Qur'anic verse at the beginning of this chapter.

Leadership is about sacrifice and paradigm shifts. Muhammad challenged the worldview of *jahiliyyah* and encountered many obstacles. Jesus, Noah, Moses, Lot, Abraham were beloved by Allah, but this did not make them immune to suffering. Syed Qutb and Malcolm X paid with their lives, but never backed down. Muhammad Ali lost his world boxing title, even though his conviction was eventually overturned by the U.S. Supreme Court. Anwar Ibrahim spent years in jail and paid with his reputation and health. Challenging the status quo is never easy, but reaching the vision outlined by your strategic plan may demand no less of you. In a hadith narrated by Abu Sa`id Al Khudri and Abu Hurayrah and reported in *Sahih al-Bukhari* (hadith no. 7.545), the Prophet said:

> *No fatigue or disease, no sorrow or sadness, no hurt or distress befalls a Muslim, even if it were the prick he receives from a thorn, but that Allah expiates some of his sins for that.*[11]

2. **Inspiring a Shared Vision**

When challenging the status quo, you need to have a vision of what you want your organization to accomplish. This is your main task. As discussed in chapter 4, this vision is the source of your organization's mission statement and long-term strategy.

In addition, you must involve your members and increase their commitment to the vision. Engaging in *shura* can help fine-tune the vision. You can also pray *salat al-istikhara* (see page 158) to ask Allah to validate the content and direction of the organization's future direction.

Once the vision is developed, effective leaders work to commit themselves to it and then to communicate it to others so

11

STRATEGY: LEADERSHIP FIT

> Imam Ali said: "Gather honest, truthful and pious people around you as your companions and friends. Train them not to flatter you, and not to seek your favor by false praises."

that they can share it and align themselves with it.[12] The general idea is to share your vision with your organization's members in order to increase their commitment to its implementation. To help others share the vision, explain it to them using "simple images or symbols or metaphors that communicate powerfully without clogging [...] communication channels [...]."[13]

3. **Enabling Others To Act**

Followers do not succeed (or fail) by themselves. They need servant-leaders, namely, leaders who are not so preoccupied with their self-serving ambitions that they cannot place other people's interests above their own.[14] If a person is using an Islamic organization for self-promotion rather than to enable others to lead, he/she can cause serious damage. In a hadith reported in *Al-Tirmidhi* (hadith no. 1345), Prophet Muhammad said: "Two hungry wolves let loose among sheep are not more destructive to them than a man's greed for property and self-aggrandizement are to his faith."[15] Note that the follower can also be a "hungry wolf" in sheep's clothing. This is what Imam Ali was stressing when he wrote to Malik al-Ashtar:

> *Never take counsel of a miser, for he will vitiate your magnanimity and frighten you of poverty. Do not take counsel of a coward also, for, he will cheat you of your resolves. Do not take counsel of the greedy too: for he will instill greed in you and turn you into a tyrant. Miserliness, cowardice and greed deprive man of his trust in God. The worst of counselors is he who has served as a counselor to unjust rulers and shared their crimes.*[16]

As a Muslim leader, you need to have the right intention (*niyyah*). Are you truly leading this organization, or just holding on desperately to a leadership position because you are the founder? If you are the former, focus on helping those around you succeed without being concerned about your own personal gain or prestige. If you are the latter, step down; there are so many other opportunities to do good work for the cause of Allah. You will learn how good your followers are only when you give them the freedom to succeed and become a servant-leader.

Servant-leaders are transformational leaders who actively foster collaboration by serving. Your hard work, and the help provided by your followers, makes things happen. To build collaboration among your members, promote frequent interaction. Hold a membership meeting every two weeks. If organizational participants are geographically dispersed, hold a conference call at least once a month. Kouzes and Posner point out that some organizations with superior leaders hold a staff meeting every morning, although this may not be feasible or even desirable in all situations.[17] By stressing superordinate (organizational) long-term goals and payoffs over short-run objectives and benefits, seek to remove any kind of *strategic myopia* that causes your followers to emphasize their functional, departmental, or committee goals at the expense of the organization's goals. Ensure that your organization's reward system promotes teamwork over individualistic efforts. Finally, foster collaboration by nurturing trusting relationships between yourself and your members, provided that you have selected them with care.

Trusting your followers to resolve problems will energize them and enable them to come up with solutions that you may never have imagined. Members must be able to see their work as meaningful and significant, and must be encouraged to take ownership of a task or a responsibility. An excellent example of what members can do when entrusted with responsibility comes from Motorola.[18] From 1987-92, this global company trained its workers to focus on quality. Hosain Rasoli, a technician involved with power transformers, had often asked himself how the transformers performed in the field. As part of the program, he was entrusted with improving the transformers' quality. After gathering information about the weakest components, he convinced the development engineers to redesign the parts. This resulted in a 400 percent improvement in product reliability. Rasoli is now Motorola's Mr. Power Amplifier

Besides fostering collaboration, you have to strengthen others through empowerment and delegation. Both concepts share the same idea: power is an *expandable resource*. The more power you share with your members or employees, the more power you have and the more you have strengthened them. This is the core of transformational leadership. In strengthening others, you are

> The more power you share with your members or employees, the more power you yourself have and the more you have strengthened them.

placing yourself in their shoes and stepping into their reality. Consequently, any demand that you make of them is a demand that you make of the whole group or organization. Muhammad was a leader who joined others in doing what he asked them to do. For example, he helped to build his mosque in Madinah, helped out around the house, and participated in the digging of the ditch prior to the battle of Ahzab. By being willing to work with your subordinates on any aspect of a project or job, you show your lower-level employees or workers that you do not feel that only they should perform the worst and/or most difficult tasks; rather, you make them feel empowered and energized through your leadership style

While strengthening your members, work at raising their level of commitment to the cause. Delegation is critical here, for the more responsible they feel for a course of action, the more committed they will become. Some leaders use a "signing up" ritual, whereby a person agrees to do his/her best.[19] Another way of building up their commitment level is by making choices visible to others. Just as at Aqaba, where the Muslims pledged their loyalty to the Prophet in public, have the Muslim brother or sister commit to performing a task in front of the group or committee. The more visible the choice, the more committed people will be to that course of action. On the other hand, guard against too much attachment to a previous course of action. Muslims who have committed themselves to a previous task may pursue it even if the project is not working out and they keep receiving negative feedback.[20] If a member becomes too attached to a continuously underperforming project, rotate him/her out and assign somebody else to it.

Once you have delegated a task, the member may not be able to carry it out. You should make sure to provide him/her with feedback designed to improve his/her performance in the future. Fight your desire to reprimand your follower immediately, for according to Kouzes and Posner, the best leaders allow their followers the space and time to learn from their mistakes, whenever feasible.[21] Islam concurs with this approach, as indicated by the Qur'anic verse revealed after the near-defeat of Uhud:

> *It is part of the Mercy of Allah that you do deal gently with them. Were you severe or harsh-hearted, they would have broken away from about you; so pass over (their faults) and ask for (Allah's) forgiveness for them; and consult them in affairs (of moment). Then when you have taken a decision put your trust in Allah. For Allah loves those who put their trust (in Him).* (Qur'an, 3:159)

Similarly, Aisha narrated and al-Tirmidhi reports, that Muhammad stated

> *Avert the infliction of prescribed penalties on Muslims as much as you can, and if there is any way out let a man go, for it is better for a leader to make a mistake in forgiving than to make a mistake in punishing.*[22]

4. ***Modeling the Way***

Your task is not done after developing a shared vision and empowering others, for now you must lead by modeling the way. First, be clear about your beliefs. By practicing what you preach, clarify to your followers what core values and behavior should be emulated. The Prophet did this, and all current Muslim leaders and followers should follow his example. By using the word *khuluq* (a derivative of *akhlaq* [ethics]) to characterize Muhammad, Allah describes our beloved Prophet as a timeless, virtuous model for all:

> وَإِنَّكَ لَعَلَىٰ خُلُقٍ عَظِيمٍ

> *And you stand an exalted standard of character.* (Qur'an, 68:4)

> The leadership model in Islam is centered around *akhlaq* or ethical behavior.

While modeling the way, remember that the level of your followers' maturity will affect the degree and speed at which they follow your example. Given the different levels of member maturity and the nature of the task, break goals down into small, manageable chunks so that you can achieve small wins. These wins are important, because they give your members self-confidence and thus have a multiplier effect.[23]

11
STRATEGY: LEADERSHIP FIT

An effective Muslim leader never loses hope in his Creator and inspires hope in others.

5. **Encouraging the Heart**

   Succeeding in Allah's Path is difficult, and Muslims will be continuously tested. Sometimes, brothers and sisters may become discouraged because a strategic plan may look too hard or is taking too long to implement. An appropriate verse or hadith from you during tough times will help them refocus and strengthen their resolve. You, in your capacity as the leader, can never lose hope in Allah, because doing so is tantamount to disbelief. The following admonition from Prophet Ya`qub illustrates this aspect of Islamic leadership:

   يَبَنِيَّ ٱذْهَبُواْ فَتَحَسَّسُواْ مِن يُوسُفَ وَأَخِيهِ وَلَا تَايْـَٔسُواْ مِن رَّوْحِ ٱللَّهِ ۖ إِنَّهُۥ لَا يَايْـَٔسُ مِن رَّوْحِ ٱللَّهِ إِلَّا ٱلْقَوْمُ ٱلْكَٰفِرُونَ ۝

   O my sons! Go and inquire about Joseph and his brother, and never give up hope of Allah's Soothing Mercy. Truly, no one despairs of Allah's Soothing Mercy except those who have no faith. (Qur'an, 12:87)

   Another inspiring verse is:

   وَلَا تَهِنُواْ وَلَا تَحْزَنُواْ وَأَنتُمُ ٱلْأَعْلَوْنَ إِن كُنتُم مُّؤْمِنِينَ ۝

   So lose not heart or fall into despair, for you must gain mastery if you are true in faith. (Qur'an, 3:139)

   A thank-you plaque (with the name of the person spelled correctly!), a dinner to thank everybody, or at the very least a nice card are all very simple but effective ways to thank your members or followers. People do not work in God's Cause with a desire to do a bad job or lose. It is up to you to show them that they can win with His help.

   No matter what, encourage your followers before the project is completely finished. One of the most important tenets of motivation is the "law of effect": Behavior that is rewarded will be repeated; behavior that is not rewarded will not be. Accordingly, establish targets along the path to a long-term objective. Whenever your members achieve a target, make it a point to celebrate their accomplishment so that they will be energized to tackle the next segment of the objective or the strategic plan.

CHAPTER 12

IMPLEMENTING THE STRATEGIC PLAN: STRATEGY–STRUCTURE FIT

An appropriate structure can channel organizational efforts during strategy formulation and implementation.

So Moses' father-in-law said to him, "The thing that you do is not good. Both you and these people who are with you will surely wear yourselves out. For this thing is too much for you; you are not able to perform it by yourself. Listen now to my voice; I will give you counsel, and God will be with you: Stand before God for the people, so that you may bring the difficulties to God. And you shall teach them the statutes and the laws, and show them the way in which they must walk and the work they must do. Moreover you shall select from all the people able men, such as fear God, men of truth, hating covetousness; and place such over them to be rulers of thousands, rulers of hundreds, rulers of fifties, and rulers of tens. And let them judge the people at all times. Then it will be that every great matter they shall bring to you, but every small matter they themselves shall judge. So it will be easier for you, for they will bear the burden with you. If you do this thing, and God so commands you, then you will be able to endure, and all these people will also go to their place in peace. (The Bible: Exodus 18:17-23. *The Bible, New King James Version,* Nashville, TN: Thomas Nelson Publishers, 1982).

For the organization to implement its strategic plan, allocate positions and resources effectively. Allocating tasks and responsibilities, as well as any associated resources, is done through the organization's structure.

12

STRATEGY: STRUCTURE FIT

As seen in the above Biblical passage, an appropriate structure can relieve much of the overload associated with implementation. The strategy and the structure must fit within the parameters to be discussed in this chapter. Initially, when setting up a new organization, its structure is likely to be a function of its strategy. Over time, though, the organization's strategy may be constrained by the previously adopted structure and the bureaucratic inertia that may have emerged since. Another point that must be considered is that a tight fit between strategy and structure is not always optimal. Pockets of a looser fit within the organizational structure may be designed in order to cushion the impact of external environmental jolts upon the organization. A fit between your organization and its external environment that is too tight may lead to a domino effect, for a major external shock can penetrate organizational boundaries without any internal buffering.

Defining Organizational Structure

Structure can be described as the sum total of the ways in which an organization's labor is divided into distinct activities and the coordination to be achieved among them.[1] Actually, structure cannot be seen; one can only see it as represented in an organizational chart. Structure describes the formal reporting relationships among organizational members, including the number of levels in the hierarchy and the span of control (e.g., how many members per chapter president, or how many salespeople per sales supervisor). Structure also characterizes jobs and the pattern among jobs in an organization.[2] It depicts the grouping of individuals into roles (e.g., supervisor vs. salesperson), roles into departments, departments into divisions, and divisions into organizations, and designates the vertical and horizontal linkages among functional departments, customer groups, or even geographical areas.

> Structure is the sum total of the ways in which an organization's labor is divided into distinct activities, and the coordination to be achieved among them.

According to Daft,[3] organizations have multiple structural dimensions, such as:

- Formalization: The amount of written documentation and procedures in the organization.
- Specialization: The degree to which tasks are segmented into eparate jobs.
- Standardization: The extent to which similar work activities are performed in a consistent, uniform manner.
- Hierarchy of authority: Who reports to whom and the span of control.

- Centralization: The hierarchical level that has the authority to make a decision. Centralization also looks at the degree to which authority is concentrated in an organization and where.
- Professionalism: The employees' level of formal education and training.
- Personnel ratios: The allocation of people to various functionsand departments.

A Contingency Approach to Organizational Design

When you start to design your organization's structure, take into account a number of contingency or situational variables. The contingency approach[4] suggests that your organization's structure depends on several variables, including size, the type of technology in place, and the level of turbulence in the external environment and strategy. Specifically:

> There is no one best structure for all organizations.

- Size is the organization's scale of activities, as reflected in the number of employees and/or members, total sales, the number of registered members, and so on. The definition of size varies according to the type of industry in which the organization is involved. How large is your mosque? Should you measure it by the square footage of the physical building, the number of Jumu`ah attendees, or the number of people at the Eid prayers? Depending on which criterion you use, you may assess your organization's size quite differently.
- Organizational technology is the nature of the production subsystem, including actions and techniques used to change organizational inputs into outputs. Technology includes not only machinery, but also work procedures, employee training and education, and other elements. According to Perrow,[5] technology can vary from routine (low number of exceptions encountered in the workflow, high number of standard operating procedures for the exceptions encountered) to non-routine (high number of unique situations in the workflow, low number of standard operating procedures for the unique situations encountered). If you own a Muslim business engaged in developing software, you are probably using a non-routine technology. Conversely, if you are operating a sugar refinery, you are likely using standardized, routine technology.
- The environment includes all elements (e.g., competitors, suppliers, customers, and governmental watchdogs) outside the organi-

12
STRATEGY: STRUCTURE FIT

zation's boundary. The environment can vary from relatively stable to relatively unstable or turbulent. It is important to realize that the environment which you perceive and plan for may not correspond to the objective environment, and that, as a result, the organization's strategies and responses to environmental forces may be flawed. An organization can adapt its structure to increasing environmental uncertainty by shifting from a mechanistic to an organic structure.[6] A mechanistic organization tends to be bureaucratic and centralized, one in which tasks are specialized and rules and the chain of command are emphasized. By contrast, an organic structure is relatively more flexible, has fewer levels in its hierarchy, and is decentralized. Tasks are not set, few rules are used, and little emphasis is placed on the chain of command.

- Goals and strategy. These were defined in earlier chapters. You can seek to control the external environment through various strategies, for example, establishing favorable linkages with important elements, buying a controlling interest in another company or acquiring it outright, or merging with one or more organizations. Organizations use different strategy types. According to Porter,[7] they can either differentiate themselves via a key attribute (e.g., quality, design, innovation, or service) or sell at the lowest possible price (i.e., be a cost leader). Some organizations can follow a best-cost approach by combining a differentiation strategy with a cost-leadership approach. In the car industry, Lexus and Mercedes follow a differentiation strategy, whereas Hyundai and KIA follow a cost-leadership approach. Meanwhile, Toyota and Honda follow a best-cost strategy (excellent quality at a reasonable price). Islamic businesses follow similar strategies; just look at Hajj travel packages (premium, low cost, or best cost). The strategy your organization chooses will determine what structure is appropriate for it.

Types of Organizational Structure

When designing your Islamic organization's structure, whether for-profit or not-for-profit, you should realize that there are different types of structure and that you need to take your situational context into account, including your strategy, before grouping people into roles and hierarchical levels. In general, your strategy, the type of environment that you face dynamically, the size of your organization, the technology you intend to use (viz., methods and processes, not just mechanical or computerized implements), the culture of your organization (and possibly of your country) determine what structure you will use initially. You need to choose wisely, because once you have settled on a structure it is quite difficult to redesign the organization.

We will discuss several types of organizational structures here, but be aware that there are many more. Ultimately, your strategy and the ensuing performance should be what guide you in designing your organization. The structures outlined by Daft,[7] Bedeian and Zammuto,[8] Duncan[9] Mintzberg,[10] which we will briefly discuss here, are classified as functional, divisional, hybrid, matrix, and dynamic network structures. Other structures exist, such as amoeba-like structures and heterarchies, but they tend to exist in very fluid environments and often across transnational borders. Thus, they do not apply to the majority of Islamic organizations.

Functional Structure

A functional structure (see figure 6) groups people and jobs by functional area. Each functional area (e.g., finance, accounting, and marketing) performs specific activities that contribute to the overall organizational process or value chain. From a contingency perspective, a functional structure is most appropriate when:

> A functional structure groups people and jobs by functional area, and focuses on internal efficiencies within each functional area.

- The external environment is relatively stable, with few, slow changes.
- Internal efficiencies within each functional area are emphasized.
- In-depth skill development within functional areas is encouraged
  This occurs as personnel within each area have the opportunity to work with multiple customer groups, products, or services.
- Functional area goals must take precedence over customer or service goals.
- The organization is small in size, produces few products or services, or works with a limited number of different customer groups (e.g., students and community group members).
- The work is routine, the technology used is well-understood, and there are few exceptional issues or problems.

On the other hand, functional structures have difficulty handling innovative strategies, change-oriented cultures, turbulent environmental forces,

12
STRATEGY: STRUCTURE FIT

and non-routine technologies. Under these circumstances, decisions that cannot be handled at the lowest level of the chain of command will be referred to the organization's functional managers or even to the president/CEO. Too many such decisions may then overload the hierarchy, causing a dramatic slowdown in operations.

Figure 6
Funcrional Structure

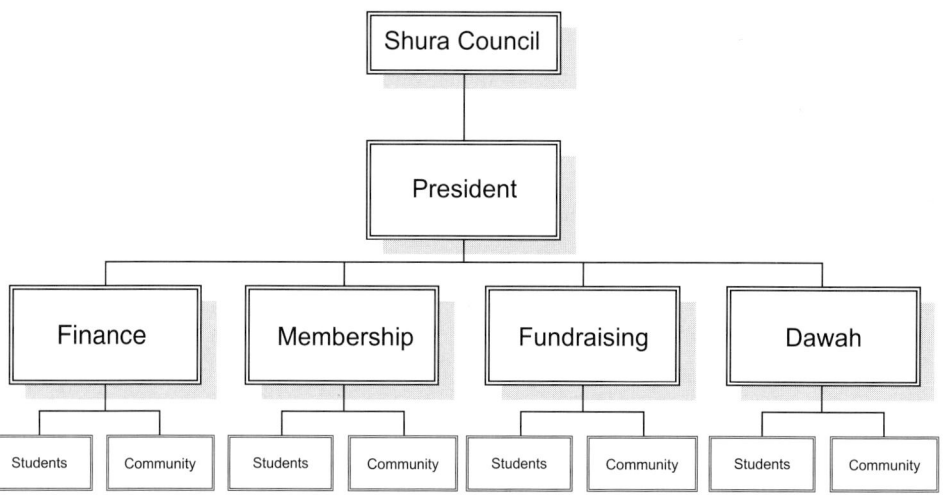

[From *Organization Theory and Design*, 3rd edition by Richard Daft. (c) 1989. Modified and reprinted with permission of South-Western, a division of Thomson Learning: www.Thomsonrights.com. Fax 800-730-2215.]

Divisional Structure

A divisional structure groups departments around products, services, customer groups or even geographical areas, and focuses on external customer responsiveness.

As shown in figure 7, in a product or customer group structure (divisional structure), departments are grouped around organizational products, services, or customer groups. Divisional structures can be quite large, incorporating many products, services, or customers. They also tend to fit the following situational context: environments that are moderate in uncertainty, strategies that focus on customer responsiveness, and technologies that are either routine or non-routine. In general, they allow the Islamic organization to deal smoothly with rapid change because of good coordination across functions. However, since departments are duplicated under each customer or product group, this increase in customer responsiveness comes at a price: decreased efficiencies in functional departments and increased operating costs.

Other advantages of a divisional structure are the following:

- Better coordination will take place among functions located under each customer or product group. However, functional coordina-

110 Strategic Planning and Implementation for Islamic Organizations

tion among customer groups or products may be hampered, since you have to go up the chain of command to the manager of the next customer or product group before being able to communicate with employees in that section. This weakness can be alleviated by establishing gangplanks across customer or product groups, namely, lateral communication channels that bypass the chain of command.

- Each customer or product group is a self-contained division (e.g., the students' or the communities' customer group). Each group's functional areas need to be autonomous, for such self-sufficiency allows each division to adapt to differences in products, regions, and customers. But this may decrease technical expertise, since employees are working on only one group of customers or one product group at a time.

Figure 7
Divisional Structure

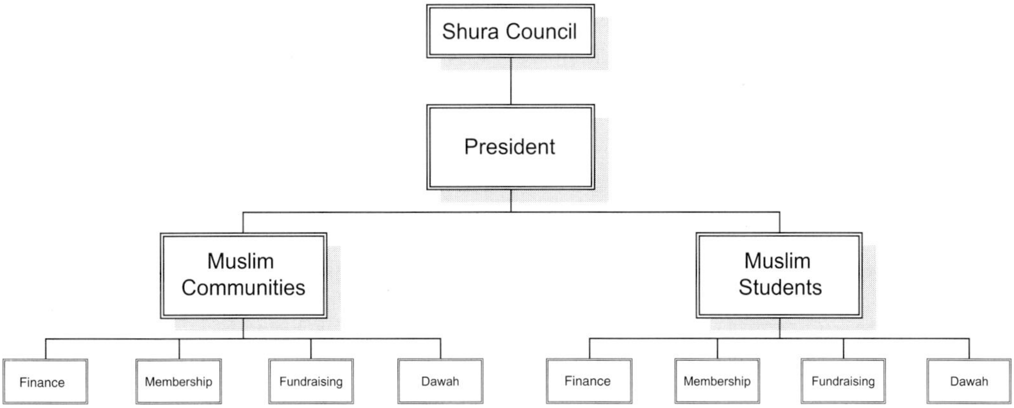

```
                    Shura Council
                         |
                     President
                    /         \
          Muslim Communities    Muslim Students
         /   |    |    \        /   |    |    \
   Finance Membership Fundraising Dawah  Finance Membership Fundraising Dawah
```

[From *Organization Theory and Design*, 3rd edition by Richard Daft. (c) 1989. Modified and reprinted with permission of South-Western, a division of Thomson Learning: www.Thomsonrights.com. Fax 800-730-2215.]

- Customer satisfaction is enhanced, because each division is responsible for a single customer group or product. Hence, contact points between the customer and the responsible division are unambiguous.

Geographical Structure

Geographical structure (see figure 8) is another type of divisional structure characterized by a grouping together of its functions according to the geographic area in which they are located. Its advantages and disadvantages are similar to those of the product structure, with the additional advantage of local responsiveness. In other words, the products or services within each geographical area will be customized to fit the needs of that area's customers. This feature is important if the customer needs across geographical regions are not similar. If they were the same globally, a regular divisional structure or product structure may suffice.

**Figure 8
Geographical Structure**

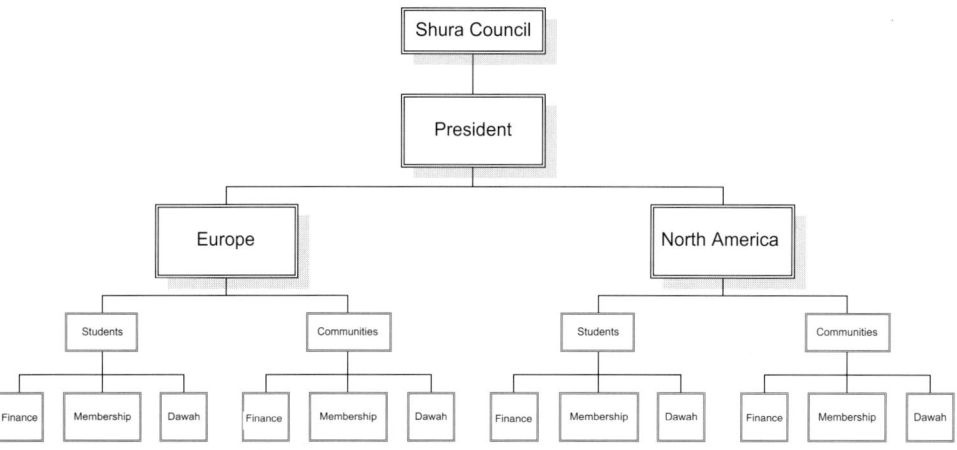

[From *Organization Theory and Design*, 3rd edition by Richard Daft. (c) 1989. Modified and reprinted with permission of South-Western, a division of Thomson Learning: www.Thomsonrights.com. Fax 800-730-2215.]

Hybrid Structure

A hybrid structure attempts to combine other structures in order to achieve efficiencies within its centralized functions and external effectiveness in its decentralized functions.

A hybrid structure (figure 9) contains elements of both a functional and a product organization:

- Some functional departments that are relevant to specific customer groups or products are decentralized and grouped together under each product or service area. The two examples we have used here are marketing and logistics.
- The remainder of the functional departments that provide services to the entire organization are centralized and usually located at the corporate headquarters (figure 9). The departments that we have included as examples are legal, membership, tarbiyyah (education), and finance.

The hybrid structure is a balance between a pure divisional and a pure functional structure that combines the advantages of each, namely, efficiency within the centralized functions that provide services to the entire organization, as well as customer responsiveness in the functional departments that are unique to each customer group and therefore located in self-contained units. Its strengths and weaknesses are a combination of the advantages and disadvantages of both functional and divisional structures.

Figure 9
Hybrid Structure

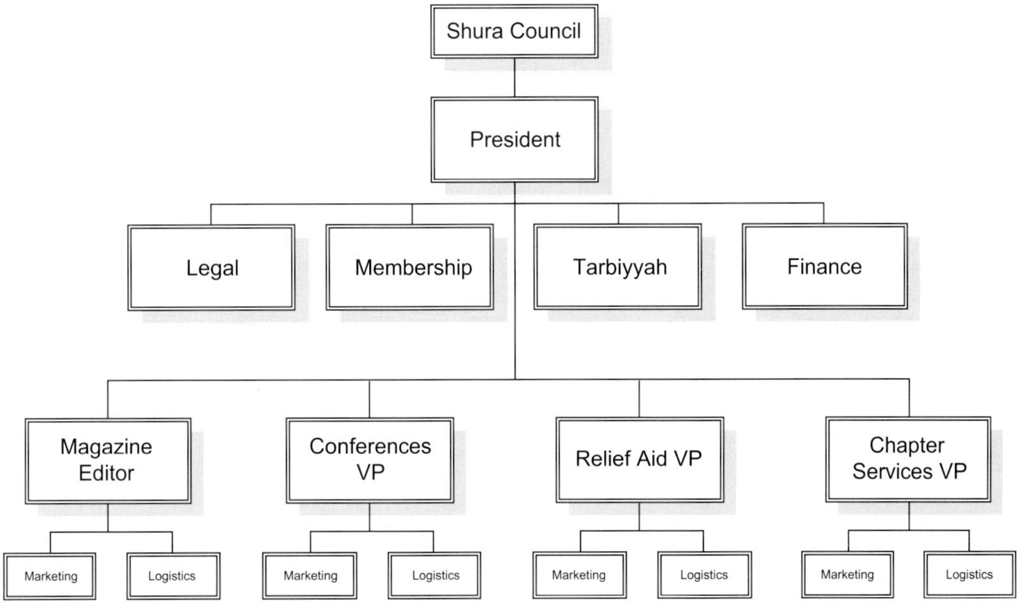

```
                        Shura Council
                             |
                         President
     _____
     |              |              |                   |
   Legal       Membership       Tarbiyyah           Finance
                             |
  _____
  |                  |                    |                 |
Magazine         Conferences          Relief Aid VP      Chapter
Editor              VP                                  Services VP
  |                  |                    |                 |
Marketing/       Marketing/           Marketing/        Marketing/
Logistics        Logistics            Logistics         Logistics
```

Matrix Structure

A matrix structure combines divisional and functional designs (figure 10) into a matrix team by bringing together personnel and resources across all functional areas and divisions (e.g., customer groups, product groups, or geographical areas) *simultaneously*.[12] This unique organizational design must meet the following three conditions to succeed:

- Flexible allocation of resources across customer groups or products. In figure 10, an employee from the finance sector may be needed in two or more matrix teams (one for students and one for communities), and may serve an equal amount of time in each team. At other times, he/she may spend 100 percent of his/her

STRATEGY: STRUCTURE FIT

> A matrix structure is sometimes called 'management by conflict', but works well when both internal efficiencies and external effectiveness are required, and when flexible allocation of resources are critical. It is one of the more challenging structures to implement.

time in matrix team A, and none in B, and later the situation may be reversed. This flexibility of moving resources to where the immediate need is, is a unique strength of a matrix structure. Should there be another group whose needs must be served by the organization (e.g., refugees), a third matrix team C can be set up overnight with human and other resources being moved from each functional area to the new team.

- Environmental pressure is essential for success on two or more critical factors, such as internal efficiency (economies of scale within each function) and external effectiveness (customer responsiveness). If there is less external pressure for customer responsiveness, the matrix will collapse into a functional structure. Conversely, if there is less external pressure for internal efficiency, the matrix will collapse into a divisional structure.

- The environment is fast moving and uncertain, and the core technology (methods and processes) is unique or not yet well understood. Matrix structures, unfortunately, tend to work well in smaller organizations with few customer or product groups.

Figure 10
Matrix Structure

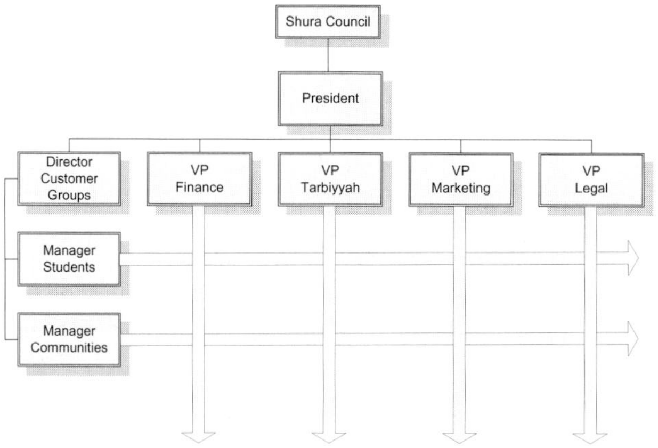

```
                        Shura Council
                             |
                         President
    ┌──────────┬──────────┬──────────┬──────────┬──────────┐
  Director      VP         VP         VP         VP
  Customer    Finance   Tarbiyyah  Marketing    Legal
   Groups
     │
  Manager
  Students
     │
  Manager
  Communities
```

[From *Organization Theory and Design*, 3rd edition by Richard Daft. (c) 1989. Modified and reprinted with permission of South-Western, a division of Thomson Learning: www.Thomsonrights.com. Fax 800-730-2215.]

The matrix relies on three key roles:[13]

- The top leader (president or CEO) must keep a balance of power between the two structures, because people within the matrix teams are answerable to two or more bosses simultaneously.

- The matrix bosses (product or customer group managers and functional area managers) must delineate their responsibilities. They need to step into the reality faced by their counterpart in the organization's other, parallel structure. In other words, a functional area manager (e.g., legal) who typically focuses on being resource-efficient now needs to understand the needs for customer responsiveness that the manager in charge of communities emphasizes on a daily basis.
- The two-boss employees within each matrix team report to two or more people, depending on the number of products or projects on which they are working at the same time. More bosses often means conflicting demands. Each of the two-boss employees is lower in the hierarchy than the managers to whom he/she responds, but acts as a liaison between the two parallel structures. His/her goal is to make his/her bosses (either functional managers or customer group managers) understand the overall need for a joint optimization of two sets of goals that appear to be antithetical (i.e., internal efficiencies and external effectiveness [customer responsiveness]).

The matrix structure has several strengths and weaknesses. For example, it:
- Achieves the degree of coordination necessary to meet dual demands (efficiency from the functional side of the organization and customer responsiveness from the divisional side of the organization). However, having two or more bosses can be frustrating and confusing to employees or volunteers.
- Provides flexible use of human resources across products. Participants need good collegial and interpersonal skills to work together smoothly.
- Is suited to frequent change in dynamic, unstable environments with innovative strategies and changing technologies. However, conflict resolution and matrix team meetings take a great deal of time.
- Provides in-depth skill development for both functional and integrative skills, but will not work unless participants are trained to use it.
- Is best in small to medium-sized organizations with several products or projects.

High-technology companies with non-routine projects in turbulent environ-

12
STRATEGY: STRUCTURE FIT

ments and with extremely innovative strategies tend to use a matrix structure. Examples include NASA, segments of the U.S. Air Force, or even a specific area of an organization (e.g., a police department's information room).

Dynamic Network Structure

A dynamic network structure[13] (figure 11), also known as a virtual organization, is a relatively new structural form. It is minimalist in nature, for the hub is the only relatively permanent and stable feature. The hub outsources various functional activities to outside specialists (e.g., product design and advertising).

> A dynamic network structure may keep costs at a minimum, but it is a minimalist structure since only the hub is permanent and stable.

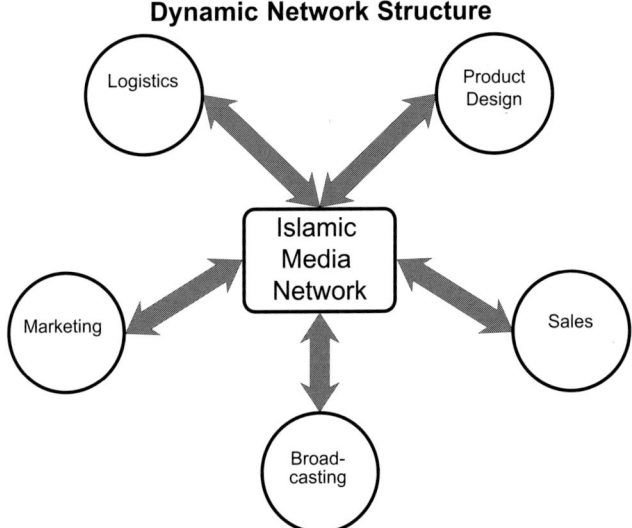

Figure 11
Dynamic Network Structure

[From *Organization Theory and Design*, 3rd edition by Richard Daft. (c) 1989. Modified and reprinted with permission of South-Western, a division of Thomson Learning: www.Thomsonrights.com. Fax 800-730-2215.]

One of the advantages of a dynamic network structure is that it keeps costs at a minimum, for there are no permanent personnel and their associated wages and entitlements do not need to be incurred by the organization during slow times. In addition, it can outsource activities to those external organizations that can best provide the service, thereby allowing those at the hub to focus on their core competencies and be flexible. A major disadvantage, however, is that the employees of these outside contractors are only temporary and do not belong to the hub. Hence, employee loyalty is non-existent. Another disadvantage is that proprietary technology or information may be compromised, since the dynamic network organization has no control over these employees once they leave the boundaries of the hub.

CHAPTER 13

IMPLEMENTING THE STRATEGIC PLAN: THE STRATEGY–CULTURE FIT

> Schein defines culture as "the accumulated shared learning of a given group, covering behavioral, emotional, and cognitive elements of the group members' total psychological functioning."

A strong culture is a prerequisite for an effective organization. Strategic plans are decided upon and implemented within the context of an organization's culture. Under conditions of environmental uncertainty, an organizational culture acts as a security blanket. "Culture" can be defined as "the accumulated shared learning of a given group, covering behavioral, emotional, and cognitive elements of the group members' total psychological functioning,"[1] whereas an "organizational culture" is a social force that controls patterns of organizational behavior by shaping members' cognitions and perceptions of meanings, and by establishing who belongs and who does not. Thus, culture involves assumptions, adaptations, perceptions, and learning.[2]

Culture also refers to the formal and informal set of values and norms that determine how individuals and groups in an organization interact with each other and with those outside. Norms are rules of conduct that the group's members establish to maintain behavioral consistency. Norms differentiate work groups from one another and promote a sense of identity and stability. Since norms are behavioral blueprints, one can expect that Islamic organizations would derive their norms from Islam. For example, a norm like "a fair day's work for a fair day's pay" is clearly related to the Prophet's hadith. In *Sahih al-Bukhari,* Abu Hurayrah reports that on the Day of Judgment, the Prophet will testify against "one who employs a laborer and gets the full work done by him but does not pay him his wages."[3]

13
STRATEGY: CULTURE FIT

Ihsan, amana, birr, and *`adl* are critical values for any Islamic organization, and the bedrock of their culture.

Values are a society's or an organization's idea about what is right or wrong, such as the belief that stealing is immoral. Islamic organizations are likely to derive many of their values (e.g., *ihsan, amanah, birr*, and *`adl*) from the Qur'an and the Sunnah. These universal Islamic values apply to all walks of life, including the corporate arena. Organizational culture may also be reflected in such organizational artifacts as heroes, stories, symbols, rituals, and language.

Typically, an organization's culture is derived, in part, from its founder's beliefs, values, and norms. In an Islamic organization, part of the culture is based on the Qur'an and the Prophet's *sirah*. For example, the Edhi Foundation's values were carefully nurtured by Abdul Sattar Edhi, its founder and president. He focuses on self-help, stating that "self-help – that's the best way to get back on your feet."[4] This message is very much related to the hadith reported by Anas ibn Malik in *Sunan Abu Dawud* (hadith no. 1637).

> A man of the Ansar came to the Prophet and begged. He (the Prophet) asked: "Have you nothing in your house?" He replied: "Yes, a piece of cloth, a part of which we wear and a part of which we spread (on the ground), and a wooden bowl from which we drink water."
>
> He said: "Bring them to me." He brought these articles to him, and he (the Prophet) took them in his hands and asked: "Who will buy these?" A man said: "I shall buy them for one dirham." He asked twice or thrice: "Who will offer more than one dirham?" A man said: "I shall buy them for two dirhams."
>
> He (the Prophet) gave these to him, took the two dirhams, and, giving them to the Ansari, said: "Buy food with one of them and hand it to your family, and buy an axe and bring it to me." He brought it to him. The Apostle of Allah fixed a handle on it with his own hands and said: "Go gather firewood and sell it, and do not let me see you for a fortnight." The man went away and gathered firewood and sold it. When he had earned ten dirhams, he came to him and bought a garment and some food.
>
> The Apostle of Allah said: "This is better for you than that begging should come as a spot on your face on the Day of Judgment. Begging is right only for three people: one who is in grinding poverty, one who is seriously in debt, or one who is responsible for compensation and finds it difficult to pay."[5]

Edhi himself is an example of self-help put in practice, for he has consistently refused large sums of money from governmental sources because "governments set conditions that I cannot accept." Another example of self-help is the large number of women trained in Edhi nursing homes in Karachi, all of whom initially had requested charity from the foundation. Edhi persuaded them to train as nurses and become independent. Those who participate in training programs receive a stipend.

Besides emphasizing self-help, Edhi also stresses parsimony and humility. In spite of handling the Edhi Foundation's $10-million budget, which comes primarily from individual Pakistanis, he lives a very simple life. "I myself am the owner of nothing, except a small 10-foot by 10-foot room that my mother left me in the alley where I first began my work, and the two sets of clothing that I wear."[6] His values, derived from Islam, are also the values of the foundation that he has run since 1951.

A Model of Organizational Culture

When developing an appropriate organizational culture, Islamic leaders may use Schein's model (figure 12) to understand their organization's culture.[7] This model is divided into three levels: artifacts and creations, espoused values, and basic assumptions.

Figure 12
Schein's Model of Organizational Culture

Level 1: ARTIFACTS AND CREATIONS
Visible, but not easily understandable to all

Level 2: ESPOUSED VALUES
People know of the existence of these values and may act in accordance to them

Level 3: BASIC ASSUMPTIONS
Actions are based on them though they are only implicit

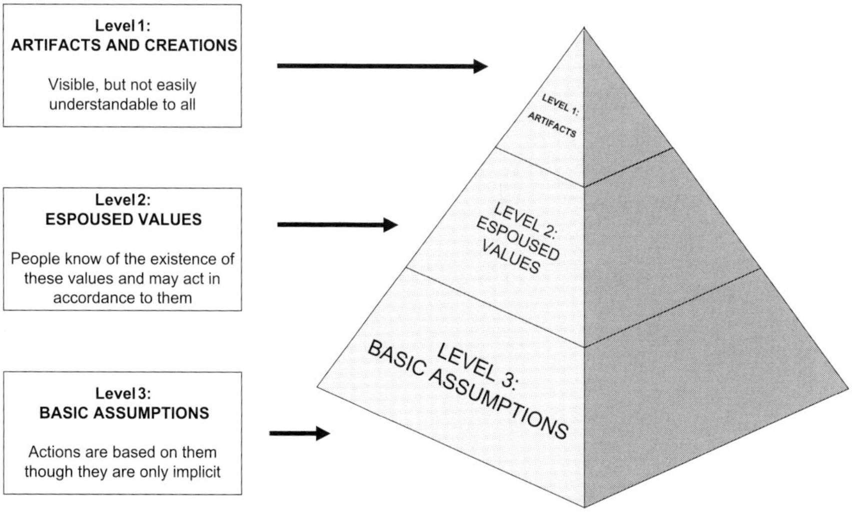

[From *Organization Culture and Leadership* 2nd edition by Edgar Schein. (c) 1997. Adapted with permission from Jossey-Bass, a division of Pfeiffer.]

13
STRATEGY: CULTURE FIT

> Schein's model suggests that culture in organizations is in three strata: artifacts and creations, espoused values, and basic assumptions.

As you and your followers progress from the organization's artifacts to its values and to the basic assumptions underlying its behavior, you progress from the visible tip of an iceberg (the artifacts) to the deepest level of the organization psyche. The first level represents the documents, letters, reports, how space is allocated according to seniority or rank, the types of office furniture, and so on. Though their meaning may not always be transparent to outsiders, artifacts are a tangible representation of the organization's values and beliefs. Is this an organization of equals, or do those who have seniority receive more respect and more perks? Does it have a Spartan culture or does it pamper those in power? Does it encourage and facilitate participation, or do the higher-ups keep to themselves and away from the lower-level employees?

A second layer represents the organization's espoused values, which often originate from its founders. For example, CAIR's central values are justice, equity, and freedom. Over time, organizational values are reinforced by stories and legends. One example is that of Herb Kelleher at Southwest Airlines, the only airline to have been profitable in America over the past ten years.

Southwest prides itself on its customer service. One story affirming the employee's belief in this value is as follows: A ticket counter agent saw, on the eve of a major American holiday, an old man walk up to the counter just after the last plane had left. The man was limping and holding some money in his hand. When the agent asked about his destination, he told her that his sister had just dropped him off at the curb, given him some money, and asked him to take a plane to his family's place. As the agent was about to mention that the last plane had just left, she noticed that blood was seeping down his pant leg. He told her that he had had surgery earlier in the day. After consulting her boss, the agent booked him on the first flight out to his destination the next day, booked him a hotel room, and booked herself a room next door in case he needed any help during the night. The next morning, she made sure that he was on the plane.[8]

Such superlative service is not uncommon at Southwest; however, it is the company's culture and values that the employees have imbibed so deeply that make these values come alive. Such organizations as IMRC and the Edhi Foundation have provided similar outstanding service over the years.

A third layer represents the organization's basic assumptions, the core values that have gradually become so ingrained that they are now implicit and taken for granted. Thus, if the company values competency, the assumption that "in the long run, one will be fairly rewarded for excellent performance" is unquestioned and employees will perform at above-average levels without being explicitly promised a reward. They know that sooner or later they will be rewarded appropriately, and this is enough to elicit their best effort.

Overall, Islam is very proactive in suggesting what the three levels of an organizational culture should be. First, with respect to artifacts, Islam encourages one to err on the side of frugality, since the money being invested in the organization belongs to the company's owners. In the case of an Islamic non-profit organization, any money raised is to be used for the purpose for which it was collected, not on deluxe furnishings or ostentatious buildings.

Umar's journey to Jerusalem illustrates Islam's emphasis on parsimony and humility. When he went to sign the city's treaty of submission, he could hardly be recognized from his small group of attendants. In fact, he went to Jerusalem only with his servant and one camel, which each of them took turns riding. When they were entering Jerusalem, the servant was riding the camel. Though the servant offered to give up his turn, Umar refused and remarked: "The honor of Islam (i.e., being a Muslim) is enough for all of us."[9] He entered Jerusalem holding the camel's rope. The Prophet and his Companions, especially Umar, were paragons of frugality. Umar's clothing was patched in many places, although he was the ruler of the Islamic state, and he used to walk Madinah's streets without a security detachment. In fact, he would often sleep alongside poor and destitute people.

Second, Islam's espoused values are straightforward. The Islamic concepts of trusteeship and work are paramount in any Islamic organization. According to the Qur'an, each person is considered Allah's *khalifah* (trustee) on Earth and human life is a test (Qur'an, 67:2). As Allah's trustee, each person's actions must be in accord with the conditions of that trust. To fulfill his/her role properly, he/she is to emulate the Prophet as the quintessential role model. As mentioned earlier, Allah uses *khuluq* to describe the Prophet's pattern of behavior (Qur'an, 68:4). This word is a derivative of *akhlaq*: ethics.[10] Hence, it can be said that the normative model of behavior for Muslims is based on ethics.

STRATEGY: CULTURE FIT

Third, a major cultural assumption in Islamic organizations relates to the concept of work. Whenever a Muslim is properly performing this work, he/she is performing an act of worship (Qur'an, 21:107, 9:34, 48:28, 61:9, and 34:28). Indeed, the Islamic concept of worship (`ibadah) is all-inclusive,[11] for any act is a potential act of worship if it is done with a pure intention and within the limits prescribed by Allah. This broader definition of worship excludes any compartmentalization of human life's various aspects. Accordingly, work (`amal) and business-related activities may be regarded as acts of worship, and therefore moral, if they meet the above two conditions. The Qur'an confirms this by mentioning `amal in more than 50 verses in conjunction with *iman* (faith).[12] Hence, the desire to please Allah through productive work can be a tremendous intrinsic motivator for Muslim workers, regardless of the levels at which they are working.

> The Qur'an mentions `amal (work) in more than 50 verses in conjunction with *iman* (faith).

This emphasis upon the individual's role as Allah's trustee and upon work as worship conditions Islam's stakeholder approach to business and is itself anchored in a multidimensional ethical system. This system, which is discussed in Beekun[13] and in Beekun and Badawi,[14] will be briefly covered in chapter 16.

The Importance of Culture

Culture can either contribute to or impede the implementation of organizational strategies. When a strategy agrees with the existing organizational values and beliefs, its implementation is facilitated. But when a strategy contradicts them, its implementation is far more difficult. Collins and Porras,[15] as well as Collins,[16] studied companies that have been consistently effective over a long period of time, and uncovered several key findings that draw attention to the importance of the culture-strategy fit.

First, they found out that the corporate cultures of these companies were built around a core set of values that functioned as their center of gravity and their compass on the way to success. Second, an organization's culture may challenge the very paradigm of strategic management because the self-examination and self-discipline implied by strategic management clashes with the organization's hitherto laissez-faire attitude.

> Because it takes so long to evolve and is so idiosyncratic, culture can become the one organizational feature that your competitors cannot copy.

Third, culture can become the one organizational feature that competitors cannot copy and can, therefore, become a source of sustainable competitive advantage. Southwest Airlines has been the most successful airline in North America for the past 15 years. Everything it does can be readily imitated: its price structure, airplane color, advertising strategy, airplane type, and so on. However, competitors have been unable to duplicate its corporate culture: its employees' dedication and fun attitude. Other examples of companies with strong corporate cultures include GE, Johnson and Johnson, Merck, and Savola. Illustration capsule 9 depicts the corporate culture of Savola, a very successful food company doing business in the Middle East. It began in 1978 as an edible oil refinery with 50 employees. Today, by the grace of Allah, it is a global diversified company with 5,000 employees, sales worth $1 billion, and doing business in several areas.

Illustration Capsule 9

Savola's Balanced Way:
A Sure Ingredient for Sustained Growth [17]

Savola Group, a Saudi group of consumer food companies with US $1 billion plus in annual revenues, has a key ingredient that is common amongst the greatest 20th century global companies such as 3M, Citicorp, Motorola, Sony, General Electric, Hewlett-Packard, and IBM (…).

The importance of a strongly entrenched corporate ideology is an aspect that has repeatedly been supported by many other business leaders. For example, David Packard, one of the founders of the global powerhouse Hewlett-Packard, has attributed the company's management outlook called *The HP Way,* as being the single most important reason for its sustained success. In his similarly titled book, *The HP Way*, Mr. Packard outlines how this ideology, which champions openness, honesty, and flexibility throughout the organization, has guided the company through 50 plus years of drastically changing environments.

Savola Group, in its business strategy, has a well defined and seemingly well practiced "core value" structure that they refer to as the "Balanced Way." This article reviews this value structure which is one of the three key characteristics […] of enduring successful companies.

13
STRATEGY: CULTURE FIT

"Balanced Way" - A Relevant Corporate Culture

What's impressive about Savola's "Balanced Way" value structure is how it derives them from Islamic ethical and moral principles and makes it pertinent to the motivations and demographics of its immediate and regional environment. For many executives, identifying and nurturing a corporate culture falls into a futile exercise of generic corporate consulting jargon. However, Savola has managed to identify a strong vision which its workforce and leadership can identify with, laying the grounds for its long-term survival and prosperity.

Savola's "Balanced Way" emphasizes a balanced approach to its corporate culture through four core ethics principles, four internal success values and four external success values.

Four Core Ethics Principles

The four core ethics principles referenced in its strategy are: *Amanah* (Honesty/Trust) that drives its commitment to its shareholders; *Taqwa* (Conscientiousness) that drives its commitment to its community; *Birr* (Caring Justice) that drives its commitment to its employees; and finally *Mujahada* (Personal Control) that drives itself toward self-improvement and self-discipline. Each of the four core-ethics comprehensively addresses all of its key stakeholders and has its origin in the Islamic code of ethics that the stakeholders can best relate to.

For example, the organization effectively applies *Amanah*, promising its business shareholders honesty in all aspects of management and in recognizing its responsibility towards its shareholders as a trust.

Four Internal Success Values

The four internal success drivers help define the values for how the organization is guided internally. These are `*Azm* (Fierce Resolve), *Iqtida'* (Apprenticeship), *Itqan* (The relentless pursuit of perfection), and, *Tawado* (Confident humility.)

These value drivers help to create an internal environment of competitive cooperation in which individuals can attain their own personal goals in the organization while taking the company forward as a whole. They create multiple dynamics to be used in various roles and relationships present in the corporate structure.

Four External Success Values
The final aspects to Savola's "Balanced Way" are the four values that drive its external success. These are *Ihsan al Dhan* (Trusting), *Iqbal* (Resonating), *Mu'azarah* (caring to help), and *Qabool* (enduring.) These values are embodied in the policies and initiatives the company has set for itself. For example – their plan to enhance corporate citizenship emanates from the value of *Iqbal*. By resonating with the needs of the external community, the Savola Group enhances its image and gives itself more opportunities to understand how to serve the needs of the community.

A Corporate Culture with the Right Motive
Savola's leadership has had the foresight to recognize the importance of being guided by its "Balanced Way" core values and to consider it as a means to raise employee morale, improve productivity, facilitate efficient decision making and ultimately ensure its long-term survival and prosperity. In doing so, it has also espoused moral standards in line with Islamic principles. The "Balanced Way" shows their willingness to admit their mistakes by drawing on the values of *Mujahada, Qabool,* and *Taqwa*. They have also incorporated the value of having the best of intentions and attribute their success to the blessings of Allah.

Of course, core values are of no value if not consistently instilled and followed. However, Savola's continued growth and profitability suggests that its leadership takes the "Balanced Way" to heart and continuously applies it to drive strategies. If the Savola Group of Companies continues to drive itself through its "Balanced Way," and continues to build upon its "core purpose," then there's no reason why in due time, it would not be placed amongst the global market leaders Nestle, Unilever, Kraft Foods, Cargill or General Mills.

13
STRATEGY: CULTURE FIT

Culture and strategy go hand-in-hand to provide competitive advantage. For this to happen, the organization's culture has to be deeply embedded in strategic thinking from the outset. This process starts, of course, with the company's vision and mission statement. For example, Savola's vision is "to build a leading publicly listed diversified investment group in the Middle East based on Savola's "Balanced Way" corporate culture."[18] Its mission statement also stresses a balanced expansion. Finally, its CEO and top executives have to promulgate the organization's values. For example, in Savola's 2002 annual report, Chairman Adel Fakeih stressed, in his letter to shareholders, "three values derived from our Islamic heritage" – *amanah, taqwa,* and *birr* – and adds "[we] aspire to practice the highest levels of these values in a balanced way."[19] In the 2003 annual report, his letter to shareholders constantly emphasized that the corporation's tremendous success was achieved "with the help of Allah."[20]

A Culture of Discipline

Savola's corporate culture also shows a commitment to disciplined action. All organizations have a culture, but only some organizations have discipline and few have a culture of discipline. When you have a culture of disciplined action, you are not as dependent on the chain of command. Indeed, the culture becomes the glue that provides coherence and unifies everybody's actions and thoughts.

As Collins discovered in his research, *a culture of discipline starts with disciplined people.*[21] People are critical to strategy implementation. The most perfectly laid-out strategic plan is useless unless you have the right people in place. This is why the Prophet initially spent so many years at Dar al-Arqam educating and training his earliest followers, including Abu Bakr, Umar, Uthman, and Imam Ali.

> A culture of discipline starts with disciplined people (Collins).

In a similar fashion, one of the twentieth century's most effective CEOs, Jack Welch of GE, built a management training center at Crotonville. As a result, GE went from a $15 billion company to a $120 billion company. Strategy implementation without disciplined people is a recipe for disaster. Discipline by itself, achieved through coercion and autocratic rule, will not yield leadership; rather, it will lead to manipulation and *misleadership*.[22] You only need to look at the non-democratic Islamic countries today to see the effects of coercive discipline. Develop a culture of discipline by hiring and developing people who are self-managed, and then manage the process instead of the people.

Another aspect of a culture of discipline is to stay close to your core competencies. Avoid anything that does not fit your vision, mission, or distinctive competencies. It takes discipline to say "no" to attractive, and yet inappropriate, opportunities that take you away from your strategic plan. Stay passionate about and focused on your vision. To preempt temptation, you may wish to start a "stop-doing" list. Be sure to list such mistakes as a fascination with your organization's size, megalomania, and nepotism.

CHAPTER 14

PERFORMANCE EVALUATION AND REVIEW

[For non-profits,] precisely because the bottom line is not a measure of accomplishment, everything becomes a moral absolute.
(Peter Drucker[1])

God loves, when one of you is doing something, that he [or she] does it in the most excellent manner.
(Prophet Muhammad[2])

> Performance assessment is to an organization what roadsigns are to a driver: It enables you to assess where you are in relation to your ultimate destination.

What is not measured is rarely performed, and is even more difficult to improve upon since there are no points of reference or benchmarks against which to measure performance. A new trend in nonprofit management is the implementation of performance measures tied to SMART objectives to make accountability clear at each organizational level and to make it easier to trace problems back to their source.

This need for assessing performance is so important that the U.S. Congress has passed the Government Performance and Results Act of 1993 (otherwise known as the Results Act). First, this act directs executive agencies to prepare 5-year strategic plans and annual performance plans that relate their long-term goals and the short-term activities of program managers. Second, the act requires that each agency report annually on the degree to which it is meeting its annual performance goals and the actions necessary to achieve or modify the goals that were not met. Most importantly, each agency's annual plan must identify performance measures for each goal and program activity and discuss how the agency will verify and validate its performance data.[3]

Of course, the business world implemented performance evaluation and review long before governments rediscovered its use. Illustration capsule 10 is an excellent demonstration of what Savola learned as a result of this self-assessment process: It had made several erroneous strategic assumptions that cost it dearly in the 1990s, and that several managerial mistakes had to be corrected.

Illustration Capsule 10
Savola's 7 Erroneous Assumptions and Management Causes [4]

Savola Group in 2002, after assessing its performance from 1992-1995, stated that they had made several erroneous strategic assumptions in spite of their incredible growth and effectiveness over the years:

1. That the level of prevailing competitive activities would continue to be at around the current level.
2. That the existing "formula for success" would continue to be relevant in the following years.
3. That business plans adequately reflected funding requirements for capital expenditure and working capital.
4. Specific industry expertise could be replicated in other industries.
5. Consumers would be willing to change their consuming habits easily.
6. High quality relevant market research has bee carried out.
7. Regulatory bodies would respond to "reasonable" change requests within a "reasonable" time frame.

PERFORMANCE EVALUATION AND REVIEW

> Further probing and self-assessment led Savola decision-makers to conclude that these assumptions had resulted from 7 "management" causes for performance from 1994 to 1998:
> 1. Communication of group mission, strategy and goals from top down was not carried out with sufficient frequency, clarity and forcefulness.
> 2. The planning process in major action programs was inadequate.
> 3. The alignment of resources to the strategy and to the realities and requirements of market conditions was not optimal.
> 4. Costly systems were built long before the actual need for them arose.
> 5. Initiatives and action programs were not supported by rigorous financial and business justification showing the full cost-benefit of each.
> 6. Accountability of individuals in the current organization structure was not fully enforced.
> 7. A prevailing culture of avoidance of unpleasant realities led to extended tolerance of lax performance and complacency.

Planning and implementation are incomplete without an examination and review of the organization's performance. Leaders must continuously track performance, assess whether implementation is on track, detect performance gaps, and craft any necessary corrective adjustments. Based on the feedback obtained during the performance evaluation process, leaders must review and update the plan as needed. Finally, effective implementation of the plan must be tied to appropriate rewards.

As Migliore et al. indicate, the evaluation and control stage of the strategic planning and implementation process can be compared to setting out on a journey with a map.[5] You know what your destination (objective) is, when you want to reach it (long-term or short-term), and how to reach it (strategy). As you proceed on your journey, you will be looking for signs along the road (performance measures) to determine where you are, whether you are on track, and how far you still have to go. If you find

14 PERFORMANCE EVALUATION AND REVIEW

that you have gotten off track (performance gap), you will seek to make corrections until you get back on the right road and reach your destination. Once you get there, you will need to select new routes (strategy) to take you to newer destinations.

What would happen if road signs along your route were lacking? How would you know whether you were on the right track? How would you determine what you needed to do to get back on the right track? In fact, your organization's strategic and operational plans are incomplete unless you build in performance measures before you start implementation. Your performance measures are the road signs along the path to your vision.

What is a Performance Measure?

Performance measures let you know quantitatively:

1. How well you are doing,
2. If you are meeting your objectives,
3. If your customers and other stakeholders are satisfied, and
4. If and where improvements are needed.

> A performance measure is composed of a number (how much) and a unit of measure (what).

A performance measure is composed of a number (how much) and a unit of measure (what). A common mistake made when using performance measures is to engage in "bean counting," such as asking how many applications the membership department processed last month. This is a meaningless measure, since the number has no denominator and, therefore, no basis for comparison. A more informative measure might be something along the following line: Of the applications received by the membership department last month, how many were processed? How long did it take to process each application (as compared to the previous month)?

Measuring Performance

> Effective organizations align their objectives and resources in order to meet their mission-driven goals.

As depicted in figure 13, performance assessment is a relatively straightforward process that starts with three steps. Step 1 involves how to develop the strategic plan's mission, goals, strategies, and objectives. Steps 2 and 3 focus on developing and using performance measures.

Effective organizations align their objectives and resources in order to meet their mission-driven goals and attempt to tie their

132 Strategic Planning and Implementation for Islamic Organizations

> They attempt to tie their goals, objectives, and performance measures.

goals, objectives, and performance measures at each organizational level to consecutive levels.[6] The ultimate goal is to establish a clear set of performance measures that are clearly linked back to the organization's strategic goals and mission. Developing such a set of measures is both time-consuming and requires *shura* among your organization's various hierarchical levels and departments.

Practice A: Produce a Few Critical and Cost-effective Measures

A well-designed and effective set of performance measures needs to exhibit five key characteristics.[7]

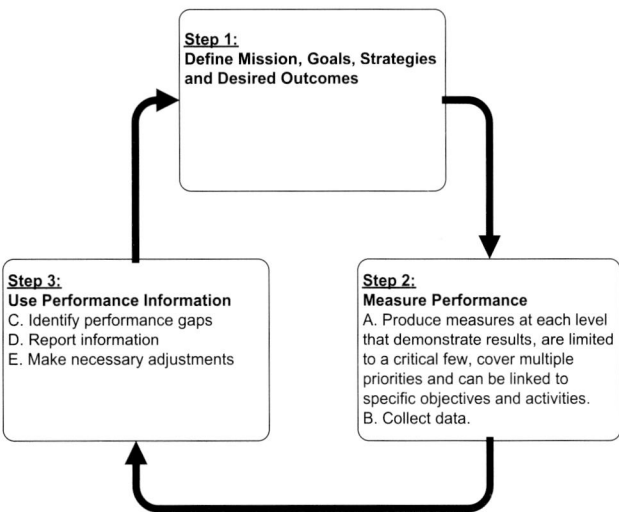

Figure 13
Key Steps in Performance Assessment

[Source: United States General Accounting Office, "*Executive Guide: Effectively Implementing the Government Performance and Results Act*" (GAO/GGD-96-118, June 1996) p. 10.]

> Use a limited, parsimonious set of relevant measures that satisfy multiple priorities simultaneously.

1. **Demonstrate results**. Performance measures must provide feedback to each organizational unit or level to show how well it is meeting its objectives and goals.
2. **Limited to the vital few.** Use a limited set of relevant measures, and make sure that your followers or employees use only a few critical measures to determine how to measure perform-

14 PERFORMANCE EVALUATION AND REVIEW

ance, locate the gaps, track down accountability, and fine-tune the organization. Too many measures are simply confusing and may involve people in so much detail that they lose track of the bigger picture. Too many measures also mean that your people are wasting valuable time measuring every detail instead of implementing that particular part of the plan.

3. **Respond to multiple priorities.** Islamic organizations often respond to the needs of multiple stakeholders that may, at times, conflict with each other. Within shar`i parameters, an organization's leader should seek to use measures that satisfy multiple priorities simultaneously, rather than just one or two.

4. **Link to responsibility centers.** Performance measures should relate to those units responsible for specific objectives and goals in order to ensure accountability and to make certain that the unit officers/leaders responsible keep in sight the outcomes they are trying to achieve.

5. **Balance ideal performance measures** and/or a large number of measures against real-world considerations. If a Muslim leader were to spend a lot of time developing the perfect performance measure or measuring the performance of anything and everything, how much incremental information would he/she really obtain from the extra effort needed to fine-tune a performance measure or analyze a forest of measures? Are his/her subordinates wasting their time measuring everything? The cost and effort of gathering and analyzing data must always be balanced against the real-world consideration of how much value is derived from the data provided by each new performance measure.

Types of Performance Measures

There are several types of performance measures, such as:

- **Input measures.** Also known as economy measures, these focus on the cost of obtaining inputs of a certain level of quality at the minimum cost, such as the cost per employee to provide a certain service.

- **Efficiency measures.** These ratio indicators of performance measure how much output is provided for a given input or how much input is used for a fixed output. This could be the number of zakah applications processed by an assessor per day or the cost per customer served and/or the time needed to serve a customer.

- **Output measures.** These consist of the quantity of the organizational, divisional, or departmental workload, as well as the work product, as part of its strategy. One example is the percentage of students enrolled in your Islamic school who graduate with a "B" average or better.
- **Outcome or effectiveness measures.** These assess whether a quality product or service that meets the needs of its intended customers or stakeholders was delivered. For example, what percentage of customers were satisfied with a service or product? In quantitative terms, how have the Muslim community at large and the general public benefited by the organization meeting its objective? What is the percentage of the Muslim community, the public, or individual customer who responded to our survey were satisfied with our products or services?

When developing a performance measure, be sure to tie them back clearly to the other elements in the strategic and operational plan (e.g., mission, goals, and objectives) at the organizational or unit level, depending on which level the measure will be used to assess performance. Table 5 illustrates how this is done.

Table 5
Linking a Performance Measure to the Strategic Plan
(Membership Unit)

Membership Unit Goal Statement	To improve the services provided to registered members.
Unit Strategy	Use web-based service request forms instead of mail-in request forms.
Unit Objective	To improve response time to members by x% within/by a predetermined time period.
Unit Performance Measure	Percent improvement in response time to members during a predetermined time period.
Linkage of the Goal to the Organization's Mission	Links to "To provide our members with an economic and timely level of service."
Linkage of the Membership Unit Goal to the Organization's Goal	Links to Organization Goal: "Maximize service delivery to membership."

14 PERFORMANCE EVALUATION AND REVIEW

Although performance measures should generally be derived from organizational or unit objectives, table 6 provides a list of sample performance measures by area for illustration purposes only. We will also discuss, in detail, practices A through E, as described in steps 2 and 3 in figure 13.

Table 6
Sample Performance Measures by Functional Area

Area to be Measured	Sample Measure
Personnel	% of employees/volunteers trained to do their job % of problems adjudicated by immediate supervisor Number of member complaints per month
Management	% of target dates attained during the last quarter % of increase in market share over prespecified time period % of revenue (or donations) generated over predefined measurement period % of improvement in customer satisfaction survey
Quality Assurance	% of time to answer customer complaints % of orders requiring corrective actions % of products/services meeting stakeholder satisfactions Number of suggestions per employee
Shipping/Manufacturing	% of customer orders filled according to specifications % of late shipments of products/services % of unplanned overtime during each quarter
Information Systems	% of time required to debug programs % of corrections on data entry
Membership or Registration	% of repeat problems corrected per month % of time improvement in correcting a predetermined number of problems % of cost in correcting a predetermined number of problems

Practice B: Collect Data

Although relevant and reliable data are critical to leaders of Islamic organizations, it can be arduous and costly to collect. Leaders will have to weigh the cost of collecting data against the need to obtain such data, and in a manner accurate enough to substantiate performance.

Invest in a good information management system, and instill a sense of discipline in implementing and gathering data until it becomes routine and automatic among the organization's members. To keep costs and time for data collection down, leaders may decide to build performance data collection directly into the daily operations rather than create a parallel and entirely new data collection system.[8] This process would be similar to the self-evaluation process that Islam encourages Muslims to engage in regularly to detect any erroneous personal behavior. Islamic organizations need to monitor themselves as they perform their work, instead of waiting for months or a whole year to do so. A small set of information-rich and built-in performance measures can help all organizations monitor and evaluate themselves.

Practice C: Identify Performance Gaps

Results-oriented Islamic leaders from some of the most effective organizations mentioned above do not stop after engaging in strategic planning and performance measurement. Rather, they use the information obtained to identify performance gaps and continuously improve their performance.

Gathering performance data is futile, unless you use it to identify the gap between the organization's actual performance and the intended level of performance. After identifying these gaps, you can see which areas need improvement and where to direct scarce resources. Since this process takes place within the context of an overall strategic plan, you can initiate actions that will keep your organization on target with respect to your overall vision and mission. When determining the size of the performance gaps, try to benchmark your organization against the best ones in your niche or area – whether secular or not, private or public. This type of comparison will enable you to understand just what your actual performance improvement potential can be and how to get there. For example, CAIR recently asked sympathetic persons of other faith-based communities to provide feedback about its website's appearance and content. The results were quite revealing and induced CAIR to revise its website's look and content.

> When determining the size of the performance gaps, try to benchmark your organization against the best ones in your niche or area — whether secular or not, private or public.

14
PERFORMANCE EVALUATION AND REVIEW

Practice D: Report Information

As the information gathered through practice C can be quite complex, it must be translated into terms that are user-friendly and meaningful to the relevant body of decision-makers: the board of directors, the *majlis al-shura*, or the executive committee. Performance reports are more helpful when they

- always report performance numbers along with the cost per output, service, or outcome achieved;
- provide longitudinal, trended data that show how the organization or unit has performed over time; and
- explain how the information gathered has been used to initiate corrective actions.

This level of accuracy and transparency is important, because then the decision-makers can make informed decisions[9] and key external stakeholders (e.g., donors, investors, members) can see the tangible link between promises and actual deliverables.

Practice E: Make Necessary Adjustments

Corrective adjustments may entail:

- Altering your organization's long-term direction and thus revisiting the organization's vision and mission. Such adjustments are rare, and should be done only when circumstances have changed drastically. Such deep, quantum-level changes may be out of your hands and require a vote from the board of directors or even ratification by a majority of your stockholders or registered members.
- Reprioritizing or reframing the organization's goals, dropping those that have become irrelevant and/or adding new ones.
- Raising or lowering performance objectives.
- Modifying strategies for certain goals.
- Improving strategy execution.

> Corrective adjustments can be both concurrent (during the current planning and implementation cycle) or long-term (during the next cycle) depending on the magnitude of the changes required.

Generally, an organization would not change its vision, mission, goals, and strategies every year. Minor adjustments may be made, unless there is a major internal or external environmental jolt. Of course, the amount of adjustment made is likely to be a function of the organization, what it is doing, the velocity of its external environment, the size of the external environmental jolts, and the unit's location within the organization.

> Recalibration is hard and Umar did not hesitate to make changes if those appointed to positions of authority did not meet his standards or if he sensed trouble ahead.

ISNA is an excellent example of an organization adjusting its goals. After years of growth, it went through a slump as the nature of services provided to its members changed. More importantly, it realized its inability to meet the needs of non-students in Muslim communities. As a result, it established a Leadership and Training Development Center to re-energize leadership in North America's Muslim communities.

Structural changes are sometimes only part of the solution. At times, the organization's leadership process itself may require recalibration. Umar did not hesitate to make changes if those appointed to positions of authority did not meet his standards or if he sensed trouble ahead. For example, he demoted Khalid ibn Walid who, along with being the Ummah's best military leader and strategist, was sometimes too harsh in his military raids and, at other times, extravagant in his tastes (e.g., for clothing and poetry). Umar removed him to preempt potential future problems. As pointed out by Altalib, Ammar ibn Yasir was a highly respected Companion who lacked any administrative savoir-faire or political savvy.[10] Although Umar made Ammar governor of Kufah, he soon dismissed him because he could not fulfill his duties effectively.

CHAPTER 15

THE CYCLE BEGINS AGAIN

> An Islamic organization will be more effective to the extent that there is fit between its strategy, structure, leadership and culture.

وَلَنَبْلُوَنَّكُم بِشَىْءٍ مِّنَ ٱلْخَوْفِ وَٱلْجُوعِ وَنَقْصٍ مِّنَ ٱلْأَمْوَٰلِ وَٱلْأَنفُسِ وَٱلثَّمَرَٰتِ ۗ وَبَشِّرِ ٱلصَّٰبِرِينَ ۝ ٱلَّذِينَ إِذَآ أَصَٰبَتْهُم مُّصِيبَةٌ قَالُوٓاْ إِنَّا لِلَّهِ وَإِنَّآ إِلَيْهِ رَٰجِعُونَ ۝ أُو۟لَٰٓئِكَ عَلَيْهِمْ صَلَوَٰتٌ مِّن رَّبِّهِمْ وَرَحْمَةٌ ۖ وَأُو۟لَٰٓئِكَ هُمُ ٱلْمُهْتَدُونَ ۝

Be sure We shall test you with something of fear and hunger, some loss in goods or lives or the fruits (of your toil), but give glad tidings to those who patiently persevere, who say when afflicted with calamity: "To Allah we belong and to Him is our return." They are those on whom (descend) blessings from Allah and Mercy, and they are the ones that receive guidance. (Qur'an, 2:155-57)

Once an organization initiates the strategic management process, it can never stop, for this is a continuous, cyclical process. As soon as the strategic plan is formulated and implemented, the SPC will initiate the data gathering for next year's cycle, and so on. Remember that, on aver-

15 THE CYCLE BEGINS AGAIN

Do not dissolve the SPC once the strategic plan is dissolved; rather, turn it into a council of advisors that will monitor strategy implementation from afar and provide advice to the Board of Directors and to the leader as needed.

age, only about 30 percent of any strategic plan is ever implemented. However, this percentage may increase over time as the organization becomes more effective at managing and directing itself in a proactive and ever-self-improving manner. Although the initial learning curve is steep and hard, organizations cannot slack off or become overconfident and lazy. They always need to stay on the alert, ready to seize opportunities and preempt threats.

In the second and subsequent iterations of the strategic management process, the SPC may decide to keep the vision and mission as they are and focus more on reprioritizing the organization's goals, strategies, and objectives. The fit between strategy, structure, leadership, and culture will always remain dynamic and require skilled tending. Use the results from the performance evaluation process to adjust the second and later versions of the strategic plan. Fix problems, not symptoms, and do so immediately so that troubled areas cannot grow and metastasize.

During the strategic management process' first iteration, the SPC must keep a full record of the discussions of the SWOT analysis and associated rankings, as well as any ideas about potential opportunities, threats, and strategies that the organization can use. Although all of these may not surface in the initial strategic plan, they may become more salient in the next year and should then be brought back and reevaluated.

The SPC's role in this ongoing process may evolve. If the SPC is dissolved, Collins recommends setting up a council of advisors.[1] This standing body, composed of people from the management team and from outside, would come from a variety of backgrounds (each member having a deep knowledge about some aspect of the organization and/or its environment), and would, if possible, meet once a week or, at the very least, once a quarter in order to gain a concurrent understanding about the issues facing the organization as it moves forward strategically.

CHAPTER 16

STRATEGY AND ETHICS

We need authentic leaders, people of the highest integrity, committed to building enduring organizations. We need leaders who have a deep sense of purpose and are true to their core values. We need leaders with the courage to build their companies to meet the needs of all their stakeholders, and who recognize the importance of their service to society.
(Bill George, Former CEO, Medtronics[1])

Whoever works righteousness benefits his own soul; whoever works evil it is against his own soul: nor is thy Lord ever unjust (in the least) to His servants. (Qur'an, 41:46)

Certainly, the best of you are those who have excellent morals.
(Muhammad [as agreed upon])

The best among the believers in faith are the best among them in character.
(Muhammad, as reported by Abu Hurayrah[2])

STRATEGY AND ETHICS

Linking Strategy to Ethics

> 'Not a soul will be dealt with unjustly in the least. And if there be (no more than) the weight of a mustard seed, We will bring it (to account) and enough are We to take account'.
> Qur'an, 21:47.

As a leader, you do not chart the organization's strategic course without being influenced by your selective perception of competitive forces, personal leadership traits, character, and personality, as well as by your ethical principles. Look at the examples of Enron, Tyco, WorldCom, and Arthur Andersen. In each case, top executives and board of director members allowed dishonest strategies to be implemented, pretended not to notice unethical behavior, or simply stole from the company. As this book goes to press, the courts are sentencing many of these crooks to well-deserved jail time and hefty fines. Ironically, some of these organizations (e.g., Arthur Andersen) were training other companies in ethics and yet paying lip-service when it came to practicing what they preached.

In contrast to these self-serving leaders, you, as a Muslim leader, should not adhere to ethical standards merely to comply with laws and regulations or to preempt a public backlash from potential misbehavior. Your Islamic organization's strategy is not truly ethical unless it can pass the deeper and more demanding moral scrutiny required of you by the Islamic ethical system.[3] One may escape the law of the land, but not Allah's omniscience and justice.

A quintessential element of the Islamic ethical system centers around the intention (*niyyah*) of the person committing an act. In the following hadith, reported in *Sahih al-Bukhari* (hadith no. 1.1) and narrated by Umar ibn al-Khattab, the importance of intention is emphasized:

> "O people! Behold, the action(s) are but (judged) by intention(s) and every man shall have but that which he intended."
> – Prophet Muhammad

> Alqamah ibn Waqqas al Laythi said: "I heard Umar, while he was on the mimbar (pulpit) delivering a sermon, saying: `I heard the Messenger of Allah say: "O people! Behold, the action(s) are but (judged) by intention(s) and every man shall have but that which he intended."' Thus he whose migration was for Allah and His Messenger, his migration was for Allah and His Messenger, and he whose migration was to achieve some worldly benefit or to take some woman in marriage, his migration was for that for which he migrated."[4]

In an Islamic organization, key decision makers such as yourself are ultimately responsible for the organization's actions and cannot hide

STRATEGY AND ETHICS

behind the legal fiction of incorporation. However, your good intentions are not enough, since they cannot, by themselves, make an unethical act ethical. Good intentions do not render the *haram* acceptable.[5] To motivate us to follow through our good intentions, Allah reveals that our actions deserve extra blessings whenever we complement our good intentions with *halal* deeds.

Figure 14
Islamic Ethics Process

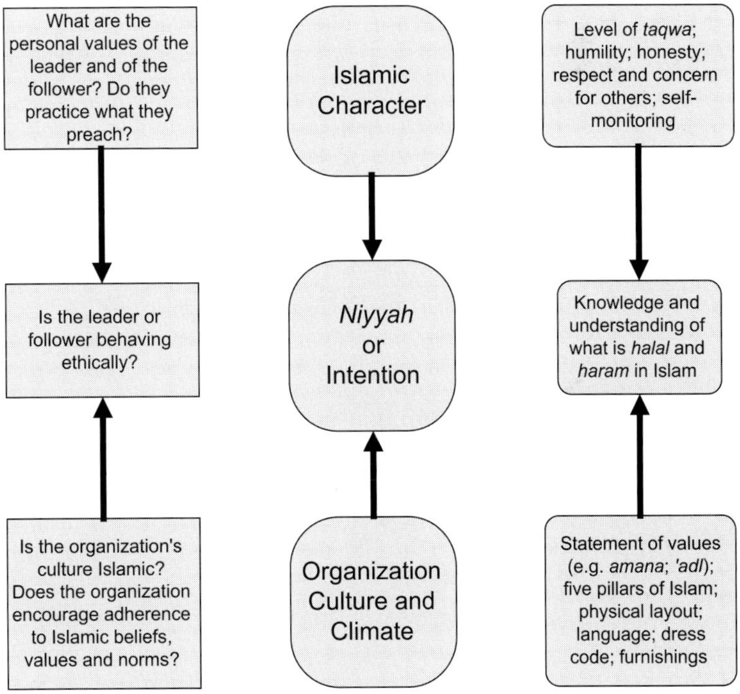

What are the personal values of the leader and of the follower? Do they practice what they preach?	Islamic Character	Level of *taqwa*; humility; honesty; respect and concern for others; self-monitoring
Is the leader or follower behaving ethically?	*Niyyah* or Intention	Knowledge and understanding of what is *halal* and *haram* in Islam
Is the organization's culture Islamic? Does the organization encourage adherence to Islamic beliefs, values and norms?	Organization Culture and Climate	Statement of values (e.g. *amana*; *'adl*); five pillars of Islam; physical layout; language; dress code; furnishings

This extra reward is clearly stressed in the following *Hadith Qudsi:*

> *Allah has written down the good deeds and the bad ones. Then He explained it [by saying that] he who has intended a good deed and has not done it, Allah writes it down with Himself as a full good deed, but if he has intended it and has done it, Allah writes it down with Himself as from ten good deeds to seven*

Strategic Planning and Implementation for Islamic Organizations   145

STRATEGY AND ETHICS

> *hundred times, or many times over. But if he has intended a bad deed and has not done it, Allah writes it down with Himself as a full good deed, but if he has intended it and has done it, Allah writes it down as one bad deed.*[6]

Islam does not allow the use of any *haram* act to achieve a good end.

Islam rewards you for your *halal* actions, but wants you to distance yourself from *haram* actions. It preempts all self-justifications that leaders engage in to condone implementing a *haram* strategy. A leader may rationalize such an undertaking on the grounds that so many people will benefit from it. However, Islam does not allow the use of any *haram* act to achieve a good end. In other words, the end does not justify the means. As the Prophet explained, if someone acquires wealth through *haram* means and then gives some of it away as charity, the giver will not benefit from it and the burden of sin will remain.[7]

Given this fact, good intentions aimed at performing *halal* actions are one layer in the ethics pyramid underlying an Islamic organization's strategy. The other two factors are leaders who have an ethical character and an organizational culture that has Islamic values. In previous chapters, as well in Beekun[8] and Beekun and Badawi,[9] we discussed both of these factors at length. I encourage you to take a look at the two books mentioned here for more detailed coverage. We will discuss only a few salient points here. Figure 14 illustrates the Islamic ethics process.

The Islamic Ethical System

Although a for-profit Islamic organization has a multi-fiduciary responsibility, Islam does not say that all stakeholders have an equal claim.

The Islamic ethical system uses a modified stakeholders' perspective.[10] In the traditional ethics literature, a stakeholder's perspective considers the claims of all stakeholders, namely, employees, management, owners/financiers, customers, suppliers, and the community, as equally valid.[11] Islam, however, recognizes the fact that the owners/financiers of your business have the right to make a profit, but not at the expense of the other stakeholders' claims. Your firm has a multi-fiduciary responsibility, but, in contrast to what Freeman proposes,[12] Islam does not say that all stakeholders have an equal claim.[13]

Owners/financiers and employees (including management) form part of a first-priority group of stakeholders, the next group includes suppliers and customers, and the final group includes all external parties. In fact, Islam suggests that emphasizing the business' moral core

STRATEGY AND ETHICS

> Islam suggests that emphasizing the business' moral core may protect, rather than threaten, the free-market system.

may protect, rather than threaten, the free-market system, for it is an act of worship (`ibadah*). An Islamically moral business can pursue its economic goals, but not at the expense of its moral obligations to society and to others affected by its actions. One example of this is manufacturing a useful product, although it pollutes the environment with waste products. Gold mining and refining makes a very useful product available, but often leads to the use of poisonous chemicals (e.g., arsenic).

Leaders of Islamic organizations must deal with several relevant criteria while engaging in strategic planning and implementation: justice and balance, trust and benevolence.

`Adl and Qist

First, the criterion of justice is described by two words: `adl* (equity and balance) and *qist* (share, portion, measure, allotment, [or] amount). In Islam, Muslims are encouraged to behave justly toward all, for such behavior is tied to an individual's very faith as a Muslim:

يَٰٓأَيُّهَا ٱلَّذِينَ ءَامَنُواْ كُونُواْ قَوَّٰمِينَ لِلَّهِ شُهَدَآءَ بِٱلْقِسْطِ ۖ وَلَا يَجْرِمَنَّكُمْ شَنَـَٔانُ قَوْمٍ عَلَىٰٓ أَلَّا تَعْدِلُواْ ۚ ٱعْدِلُواْ هُوَ أَقْرَبُ لِلتَّقْوَىٰ ۖ وَٱتَّقُواْ ٱللَّهَ ۚ إِنَّ ٱللَّهَ خَبِيرٌۢ بِمَا تَعْمَلُونَ ۝

> `Adl* applies to the concept of balance and equilibrium: doing things in a proportionate manner and avoiding extremes.

O you who believe! Stand out firmly for Allah, as witnesses to fair dealing, and let not the hatred of others to you make you swerve to wrong and depart from justice. Be just: that is next to piety: and fear Allah. For Allah is well-acquainted with all that you do. (Qur'an, 5:8)

Acting justly in this life means that one can expect similar justice from Allah in the Hereafter: "Deal not unjustly and you shall not be dealt with unjustly." (Qur'an, 2:279)

At the same time, `adl* applies to the concept of balance and equilibrium, doing things in a proportionate manner and avoiding extremes. It is a dynamic characteristic for which each Muslim must strive. This idea of balance is consistent with the concepts of equity and justice.

> *Qist* means to give every person and everything their proper due.

The Qur'an also uses *qist* for justice. As Siddiqui indicates,[14] *qist* means to give every person and every thing their proper due. Allah says "… and be fair, for Allah loves those who are fair (and just)." (Qur'an, 49:9) Thus,

STRATEGY AND ETHICS

Islam teaches that a person should be just in every aspect of his/her life to all people and things, and at all times.

As a leader, make sure that your organization's strategy is balanced and gives everyone their proper due. Profit maximization in the manner discussed by Nobel Prize winner Milton Friedman focuses on only one set of stakeholders: the owners or stockholders. Although it is against price controls,[15] Islam encourages you to earn a fair return, but not at the expense of consumers. Your employees cannot lie, swear oaths, or hide any product or service flaws, nor can they cheat when measuring out the product.

وَأَوْفُوا۟ ٱلْكَيْلَ إِذَا كِلْتُمْ وَزِنُوا۟ بِٱلْقِسْطَاسِ ٱلْمُسْتَقِيمِ ۚ ذَٰلِكَ خَيْرٌ وَأَحْسَنُ تَأْوِيلًا ﴿٣٥﴾

Give full measure when you measure, and weigh with a balance that is straight. That is the most fitting and the most advantageous in the final determination. (Qur'an, 17:35)

Amanah

Amanah (trust) suggests that we are all Allah's trustees on earth and, hence, all organizational participants bear responsibility for what they do.

The second criterion of Islamic ethics is the concept of *amanah* (trust), for we are Allah's trustees on Earth and, as such, are responsible for our actions.

كُلُّ نَفْسٍ بِمَا كَسَبَتْ رَهِينَةٌ ﴿٣٨﴾

Every soul will be (held) in pledge for its deeds. (Qur'an, 74:38)

As Ahmad indicates,[16] realizing Allah's will by behaving morally is part of our trusteeship and a responsibility that we have agreed to fulfill. More importantly, the wealth and other resources to which we have access are not ours; rather, Allah has loaned them to us so that we can act as real trustees. As we will discuss later, a company's executives are responsible for the strategies in which their company engages.

Ihsan

The third criterion of Islamic ethics is *ihsan* (benevolence, excellence, kindness to others). This term is defined as "an act which benefits persons other than those from whom the act proceeds

STRATEGY AND ETHICS

Ihsan is a multi-dimensional concept. It means excellence as well as benevolence and kindness to others. Islamic corporations and non-profit organizations need to pursue excellence but not at the expense of benevolence and kindness. Excellence in *dunya* does not imply excellence in *deen*.

without any obligation."[17] Islam encourages kindness. In a hadith narrated by Iyad ibn Himar in *Sahih Muslim* (hadith no. 6853), the Prophet said that among the inhabitants of Paradise will be:

> [...] one who wields authority and is just and fair; one who is truthful and has been endowed with power to do good deeds; and the person who is merciful and kind-hearted towards his relatives and to every pious Muslim, and who does not stretch out his hand in spite of having a large family to support.[18]

At its core, *ihsan* is derived from the Arabic root *h-s-n*, which means "suitable, beautiful, proper, or fitting."[19] This concept is the core of Islamic ethics, because it focuses on behaving in a way that pleases Allah. Your Islamic organization should be a benevolent organization, and its strategy should be to demonstrate *ihsan* without shortchanging your fiduciary responsibility to the company's owners or stockholders. Benevolence does not mean mediocrity or giving away the company's earnings gratuitously.

In addition, *ihsan* includes excellence. This ethical dimension applies to any constructive endeavor or work. Furthermore, it implies that each committed Muslim executive, board member, or employee should perform his/her work for the love of Allah in full knowledge that Allah is always watching his/her behavior, whether public or private. Within the context of strategy, should you be a manager in an organization with absentee owners (i.e., a company that is publicly traded on the stock exchange), you must do your level best to minimize agency effects. In other words, you should not act to serve your own interests when the business' owners or stockholders are not watching you. In such a case, benevolence or excellence means acting as a good steward of the organization. Islam tries to preempt agency effects by having you, your employee, or your board members monitor themselves out of their own personal desire to implement *ihsan* in their lives. This agency issue is at the heart of the ethical scandals in major multinational corporations as professional managers take advantage of the ignorance of absentee stockholders to fill their own pockets.[20]

STRATEGY AND ETHICS

Responsibility and Accountability

To meet the dictates of balance and unity that we see in Allah's creation, each person is considered accountable for his/her actions. Allah stresses this concept of moral responsibility:

لَّيْسَ بِأَمَانِيِّكُمْ وَلَآ أَمَانِيِّ أَهْلِ ٱلْكِتَـٰبِ ۗ مَن يَعْمَلْ سُوٓءًا يُجْزَ بِهِۦ وَلَا يَجِدْ لَهُۥ مِن دُونِ ٱللَّهِ وَلِيًّا وَلَا نَصِيرًا ۝

> *Not your desires, nor those of the People of the Book (can prevail): whoever works evil, will be requited accordingly. Nor will he find, besides Allah, any protector or helper. (Qur'an, 4:123)*

In Islam, responsibility is multi-layered and focuses on both the micro- (individual) level and the macro- (organizational and societal) level. In fact, Islam brings these two levels together. As Syed Qutb points out,

> *Islam lays down the principle of mutual responsibility in all its various shapes and forms. In it, we find the responsibilities which exist between a man and his soul, between a man and his immediate family, between the individual and society, between community and other communities [...].*[21]

In Islam, responsibility is multi-layered and focuses on both the micro- (individual) level and the macro- (organizational and societal) level.

Assigning responsibility for unethical strategic action is difficult in any organization for two primary reasons.[22] First, the state of current accounting and financial equivocation is such that facts are difficult to determine and dubious practices are easily concealed, as the Enron and Tyco scandals revealed so clearly. Government prosecutors and even expert analysts had difficulty seeing through the fog of the executives' deceptive practices.

Second, and in conceptual terms, an event can have multiple causes. Is the lack of ethical behavior of the executives now being prosecuted the result of the climate of greed preceding the dot-com debacle? Or, is it the fact that a repeat felon who robs a grocery store for $300 may get more jail time than a white-collar criminal who steals over $600 million from his/her company? Or, is it the American political system that survives on campaign donations from the same indicted executives? Enron, along

STRATEGY AND ETHICS

with its CEO, was one of the largest donors to the Bush reelection campaign. Or, could it be the members of the board of directors, most of whom were appointed by the very CEO whom they were supposed to monitor? Or, could it be that stockholders could not care less about what top executives do as long as their dividend check is high and regular?

Corporate character theory has toyed with the idea of assigning responsibility.[23] It states that a corporation is culpable if it adopts an illegal policy that one of its agents then endorses or executes. Such devices as standard operating procedures, decision procedures, and so on are also relevant, for their existence gives rise to a corporate character that may promote either ethical or unethical behavior. A corporation is also deemed culpable if it has a prior history of such activity, thus indicating its endorsement of earlier offenses, or if executives willfully obstruct or fail to prevent the obstruction of justice once they are caught. To make it easier to assess corporate responsibility, U.S. Federal Sentencing Guidelines actually calculate a "culpability score" for each offending organization.

Instead of trying to establish corporate responsibility, Islam rejects the idea that corporations have a collective consciousness (viz., that they are considered persons before the law) that eschews individual responsibility. Rather, Islam tends to focus on the Muslim decision maker/leader and to stress that he/she cannot blame his/her actions on the pressures of business or on the fact that everybody else is behaving unethically. Each individual bears ultimate responsibility for his/her actions (Qur'an, 74:38). No leader can dodge his/her responsibility. In a hadith narrated by Ibn Umar in *Sahih al-Bukhari* (hadith no. 7.128), the Prophet said:

> All of you are guardians and are responsible for your wards. The ruler is a guardian and the man is a guardian of his family; the lady is a guardian and is responsible for her husband's house and his offspring; and so all of you are guardians and are responsible for your wards.[24]

Hence, diffusion of responsibility and concealment under the corporate umbrella are against the spirit of Islam. Your position as leader makes you accountable in front of Allah for your actions on the Day of Judgment. Judge for yourself from the following well-known hadith narrated by Abu Dharr and reported in *Sahih Muslim* (hadith no. 4491):

Corporate Character Theory states that a corporation is culpable if it adopts an illegal policy that one of its agents then endorses or executes.

Islam rejects the idea that corporations have a collective consciousness, and that one should estalish corporate responsibility; rather it focuses on individual responsibility.

16
STRATEGY AND ETHICS

I said to the Prophet (peace be upon him): "Messenger of Allah, will you not appoint me to a public office? "He stroked my shoulder with his hand and said: "Abu Dharr, you are weak and authority is a trust, and on the Day of Judgment it is a cause of humiliation and repentance except for one who fulfils its obligations and (properly) discharges the duties attendant thereon."[25]

In other words, the Islamic ethical system demands that you and your organization's followers or employees be just, trustworthy, and benevolent; seek to achieve excellence; and accept responsibility for your actions. Doing the above with the right intention, with the realization that work is indeed an act of worship, and that you are designing and implementing a strategy that will earn you success not just in this life but also in the Hereafter fulfills your responsibility as His trustee on Earth. Hearken to Allah's injunction and promise:

يَٰٓأَيُّهَا ٱلَّذِينَ ءَامَنُواْ ٱتَّقُواْ ٱللَّهَ وَقُولُواْ قَوْلًا سَدِيدًا ۝ يُصْلِحْ لَكُمْ أَعْمَٰلَكُمْ وَيَغْفِرْ لَكُمْ ذُنُوبَكُمْ ۗ وَمَن يُطِعِ ٱللَّهَ وَرَسُولَهُۥ فَقَدْ فَازَ فَوْزًا عَظِيمًا ۝

O you who believe! Fear Allah and (always) say a word directed to the Right: that He may make your conduct whole and sound and forgive you your sins: he that obeys Allah and His Apostle has already attained the highest achievement. (Qur'an, 33:70-71)

CHAPTER 17

TAWAKKUL OR TRUSTING IN ALLAH

إِن يَنصُرْكُمُ ٱللَّهُ فَلَا غَالِبَ لَكُمْ ۖ وَإِن يَخْذُلْكُمْ فَمَن ذَا ٱلَّذِى يَنصُرُكُم مِّنۢ بَعْدِهِۦ ۗ وَعَلَى ٱللَّهِ فَلْيَتَوَكَّلِ ٱلْمُؤْمِنُونَ ۝

If Allah helps you, none can overcome you: if He forsakes you, who is there after that that can help you? In Allah, then, let believers put their trust. (Qur'an, 3:160)

O Allah, You are my lord. There is no god but You. I put my trust in You. You are the Lord of the Mighty Throne. Whatever Allah wills will happen and what He does not will cannot happen. There is no power or strength except with Allah, the Exalted, the Mighty. I know that Allah has power over all things, and that Allah comprehends all things in knowledge. O Allah, I seek refuge with You from the evil of myself and from the evil of all creatures under your control. Surely, the straight way is my Sustainer's way.

(*Du`a* of Prophet Muhammad[1])

When Abraham had differences with his wife (Sarah), (because of her jealousy of Hajar, Ishmael's mother), he took Ishmael and

17
TTAWAKKUL OR TRUSTING IN ALLAH

> Muslim decision-makers should not place unwarranted confidence in their plans and their ability to execute them; whatever they plan and do, they must put their trust in Allah. Prophet Muhammad said in a du`a, "Whatever Allah wills will happen, and what He does not will cannot happen."

his mother and went away. They had a water-skin with them containing some water. Ishmael's mother used to drink water from the water-skin so that her milk would increase for her child. When Abraham reached Mecca, he made her sit under a tree and afterwards returned home. Ishmael's mother followed him, and when they reached Kada', she called him from behind: "O Abraham! To whom are you leaving us?" He replied: "(I am leaving you) to Allah's (care)." She said: "I am satisfied to be with Allah" [...].

Narrated by Ibn Abbas[2]

As the Prophet clearly stated and demonstrated, Islam encourages strategic planning and thinking. People, however, may place unwarranted confidence in their plans and their ability to execute them. For Muslims, such one-sided confidence borders on arrogance and is dangerous because it challenges a major dimension of Islam: that of *tawakkul* (trust/reliance in Allah). Anas ibn Malik reported in the following hadith that:

> *A man once rode into town on a fine she-camel of his, and he said: "O Messenger of Allah, shall I just leave her unattended, and put my trust in the Lord [ada'u-ha wa atawakkalu]?" So the Prophet told him: "Hobble her feet with a rope and put your trust in the Lord [a'qil-ha wa tawakkal]." [3]*

No matter how good our plans are, they cannot succeed unless Allah wills them to. Allah tells us to rely on Him and to strive for our objectives (*Surat al-Jamu`ah*[10]) for He is the master planner and trusting in Him (*tawakkul*) is a sign of belief. *Tawakkul* is clearly related to *iman*, as indicated in the following verse:

ٱللَّهُ لَآ إِلَٰهَ إِلَّا هُوَ ۚ وَعَلَى ٱللَّهِ فَلْيَتَوَكَّلِ ٱلْمُؤْمِنُونَ

Allah! There is no god but He: and on Allah therefore let the Believers put their trust. (Qur'an, 64:13)

The Qur'an uses *iman* and *tawakkul* in many of its verses (e.g., Qur'an, 2:283, 4:36, 8:27, 11:56, 14:11, and 58:10). In a *hadith sahih* reported in Ahmad, al-Nasa'i, Ibn Majah, al-Hakim, and al-Tirmidhi, Umar ibn al-Khattab narrates that the Prophet said:

If only you relied on Allah a true reliance, He would provide sustenance for you just as He does the birds: They fly out in the morning empty and return in the afternoon with full stomachs.[4]

> Although trust and reliance on Allah are one of the most important causes of success in this life, they do not negate strategic planning, working, and striving for sustenance in this life.

Although trust and reliance on Allah are one of the most important causes of success in this life, they do not negate strategic planning, working, and striving for sustenance in this life. As hadith commentators (such as al-Bayhaqi) have noted, the bird is, in fact, working to support itself. It does not sit idly in its nest or on a branch waiting for food; rather, during the day it actively searches for insects and other food and trusts its Creator to feed it. Allah feeds billions of birds and other creatures every day.

In other words, *tawakkul* does not mean abandoning work or becoming a fatalist. You must plan, live your life, and work to support yourself and your family to the best of your ability. Yet having done all of these, you must never rely solely on yourself and your actions, for success is not up to you. Ultimately, you must submit to His will with complete sincerity. Your organization's plan cannot be implemented and cannot succeed unless Allah wills it.

In the same manner, your competitor's plans or those who work against Islam or Islamic organizations are futile without Allah's will. This fact is amply illustrated in the Prophet's *sirah*. During his migration from Makkah to Madinah, the Prophet and Abu Bakr could hear their pursuers' voices from inside the cave, where they were hiding. Relying completely on Allah, he told Abu Bakr: *Do not grieve, for Allah is assuredly with us* (Qur'an, 9:40). Similarly, when Abraham was thrown into the fire, he uttered the same words that Muhammad did when he was being threatened:

> For us Allah is Sufficient and He is the best Disposer of affairs *(Hasbun Allahu wa ni`mah al-wakil)*

ٱلَّذِينَ قَالَ لَهُمُ ٱلنَّاسُ إِنَّ ٱلنَّاسَ قَدْ جَمَعُوا۟ لَكُمْ فَٱخْشَوْهُمْ فَزَادَهُمْ إِيمَـٰنًا وَقَالُوا۟ حَسْبُنَا ٱللَّهُ وَنِعْمَ ٱلْوَكِيلُ ۝

Men said to them: "The people are gathering against you, so fear them." But it only increased their faith; they said: "For us Allah is Sufficient and He is the best Disposer of affairs" (Hasbun Allahu wa ni`mah al-wakil). (Qur'an, 3:173)

Allah cooled the fire so that Abraham would not be incinerated, and turned the Prophet's pursuers away with a spider's web and a rock dove's nest.

17
TTAWAKKUL OR TRUSTING IN ALLAH

Illustration capsule 11 describes the example of Hakeem Olajuwon, one of the great basketball players in the world, and his personal discovery of *tawakkul*.

Illustration Capsule 11
***Tawakkul* and the Success of One of the USA's Greatest Basketball Stars**[5]

Brother Hakeem Olajuwon taught me the importance of *Tawakkul*, or trusting Allah.

Br. Hakeem was an MVP on the Houston Rockets basketball team a couple of years ago when I first got to know him.

I remember reading before he became the star of the team, that he was a very good player but had a very bad temper. He would regularly fight with other players and swear, for instance.

Although he was a good player, his team went nowhere. But suddenly, in the mid-1990s, that changed, and the Rockets became a winning team instead of one with a couple of good players but no coordination. This culminated in their success in the 1994 and 1995 NBA championships.

Br. Hakeem used to be a non-practicing Muslim. I and a group of friends once asked him how the transformation to Islam affected his character.

"Before I started practicing my faith, I used to completely rely on myself. When I had done my best, I would be extremely frustrated if I didn't win. It would irritate and anger me. And that was causing me to be bad to others by fighting and swearing," he explained.

"But when I started practicing my faith, I learned that results are not my property. I started doing my best but then I left success and failure to my Creator. Now I was not irritated by failure and was not overinflated by success. That caused me to calm down and improve my behavior towards others on my team and we became a team."

TTAWAKKUL OR TRUSTING IN ALLAH

The difference between Br. Hakeem before and after was his understanding of the concept of *Tawakkul*, which is a major concept in the relationship of a believer with his or her Creator. When a believer fully practices *Tawakkul* by putting his or her full trust in Allah, this person realizes that they are not all-powerful, Allah is. Although we all control some variables that Allah has given us in our control, Allah ultimately controls all the other variables known or unknown to us.

Our capacities are limited. Allah's are unlimited. We are responsible for following His command by doing our duty and making a right choice in the world of choices and following them up with action. In this way, good intentions and directions combined with good steps are what we are responsible for. And as Muslims, we want to do our best in that area. But results, positive or negative, are not always in our control. They are dependent upon the laws and prophecies which Allah has put in place and on His Will.

Sometimes we think that something is good for us and actually it is bad for us. And sometimes we feel that something is bad for us while actually it is the other way around. So the limit of human knowledge explains the limits of not only our control, but our responsibility as well. That is why we do our part and leave things in terms of results to God.

Adopting the belief and practice of *Tawakkul* has two benefits for us. First, knowing that our responsibility for what happens is limited is very comforting. Those who do not realize the limits of human responsibility normally transgress on others' rights by forcing their will on them through verbal or physical violence or they may get depressed and lose their mind or hurt themselves. So it is the Mercy of Allah that He has told us that our responsibility is limited. And that is the meaning of "On no soul does Allah place a burden greater than it can bear" (Qur'an, 2:286) as well as the understanding of individual responsibility.

The second consequence of *Tawakkul* is that it invites us to connect to a powerful Ally Who is no one but the Lord Himself.

17
TTAWAKKUL OR TRUSTING IN ALLAH

> The more we rely on Him, the greater the chances that we will try to please Him by following the guidance He has given us, which in turn will lead to goodness in this world and success in the Hereafter.
>
> The third consequence of *Tawakkul* is what Br. Hakeem learned by observing himself. By fully trusting in Allah and relying on Him, we are not depressed by what we have lost or intoxicated by our success (Qur'an, 57:22-23). We know that all things are in Allah's hands. And that makes us not only humbler but more submissive to Allah, thus better believers.
>
> "And put your trust and reliance in Allah, and sufficient is Allah as a Trustee." (Qur'an, 33:3)
>
> "And trust and rely on the Living One (Allah), Who will never die, and celebrate His praises and thanks. And Sufficient is He to be acquainted with the sins of His slaves." (Qur'an, 25:58)
>
> "And whoever places his trust in Allah, Sufficient is He for him, for Allah will surely accomplish His Purpose: For verily, Allah has appointed for all things a due proportion" (Qur'an, 65:3) [...]

Salat al-Istikhara

Salat al-istikhara is a special prayer performed to ask Allah for guidance, especially when you have to choose between two permissible alternatives.

Istikhara (seeking guidance from Allah) is one of the avenues that our Creator has made available to guide those who put their trust in Him. *Salat al-istikhara* is a special prayer that you can perform to ask Allah to guide you in any affair in your life, especially when you have to choose between two permissible alternatives. As pointed out in *Fiqh-us-Sunnah* (4.41), Qatadah said: "Every people who seek the pleasure of Allah and consult with one another are guided to the best course in their affairs."[6] In the course of developing and implementing your organization's strategic plan, you will confront multiple alternatives. Prayer, especially *salat al-istikhara*, is one way that you can seek guidance from the Omniscient One.

Several hadiths point to the importance of this special prayer: Sa`d ibn Waqas reported that the Prophet said:

> Istikhara (seeking guidance from Allah) is one of the distinct favors (of Allah) upon man, and a good fortune for the son

of Adam is to be pleased with the judgment of Allah.⁷ And a misfortune of the son of Adam is his failure to make istikhara (seeking Allah's guidance), and a misfortune for the son of Adam is his displeasure with the judgment of Allah.

For more information on how to perform *Salat al-Istikhara*, please see *Sahih al Bukhari*, Volume 2, hadith 263).

Final Words

Create a world of your own
If you are amongst the living!
The secret of the creation of Adam, and the object
Of Divine Order: "Be!"
And then "It was!" – is Life!
[...]

O foolish Glow-Worm!
Get rid of revolving
Around the Lamp,
And live in the illumination
Of thy own Nature!
[...]

Never forget that you are a Muslim!
Keep your breast brimmed
With healthy longings; and
Always remember this holy Verse:
"Allah does not break
His Promise (with true Believers)"!

[Selections from Mohammad Iqbal's *Khizr-e-Raah*[1]]

APPENDIX A

STRATEGIC PLANNING AND IMPLEMENTATION WORKSHEETS

The worksheets included here accompany Professor Rafik I. Beekun's *Strategic Planning and Implementation for Islamic Organizations* and are best used in conjunction with it.

Permission to Use

If you have purchased this book, you can duplicate these worksheets within your organization. However, we ask that you do not delete the copyright notice on each worksheet.

APPENDIX-A

Worksheet #1
Selecting the Strategic Planning Committee (SPC)

Choosing SPC members is critical. Remember that SPC members need to be key stakeholders both from inside and outside the organization, add value, and be collegial in their approach. If you choose too many members, the process will be very time-consuming, potentially contentious, and hard to manage.

Name	To which stakeholder group do they belong?	What is their role in, and contribution to, our organization?	What value do they add to the SPC?

Source: Beekun, Rafik. *Strategic Planning and Implementation for Islamic Organizations.*
© Copyright: IIIT, 2006. All rights reserved.

APPENDIX-A

Worksheet #2
Putting Together a Planning Binder for the Strategic Planning Committee

A planning binder often helps SPC members initiate the strategic plan's development. If the SPC has been through this process before, you may wish to skip this list.

\multicolumn{2}{c}{Information to be included in the Planning Binder}	
Yes/No?	List of suggested items
	1. Cover sheet with title and planning schedule
	2. Rationale for conducting strategic planning now
	3. A copy of this book and/or other similar books/sources on strategic planning
	4. Selected worksheets from this book placed in appropriate sections
	5. Previous versions of the organization's vision, mission, goals, or strategic plan
	6. Relevant organizational documents: organizational history, chart, financial documents, constitution, and by-laws
	7. List relevant addresses and e-mail information, as well as each SPC member's role
	8. Expected time line for the strategic planning process
	9. People or officers who could be information resource points during the process
	10. Other material to be included in binder?

(This worksheet is partly adapted from McNamara, Carter. *Field Guide to Nonprofit Strategic Planning and Facilitation.* Minneapolis, Minnesota, 2003, pp. 240)

Source: Beekun, Rafik. *Strategic Planning and Implementation for Islamic Organizations.*
© Copyright: IIIT, 2006. All rights reserved.

APPENDIX-A

Worksheet #3
SWOT Analysis-Strengths

FOR (organization)_____

Date_____

DEFINITION: Strengths are internal to the organization. A strength is something the organization is good at or a resource that gives it an important capability, a useful competence, a critical or proprietary know-how, or a valuable organizational achievement.

Please rate each strength along a continuous scale where 5 = major strength, 4 = less major strength, 3 = average strength, 2 = below average strength, 1 = weak strength. Insert your rating in the blank column next to each strength listed below

Internal Strengths	Rating
Example: Our organization has a core group of committed members.	

Source: Beekun, Rafik. *Strategic Planning and Implementation for Islamic Organizations.*
© Copyright: IIIT, 2006. All rights reserved.

APPENDIX-A

Worksheet #4
SWOT Analysis-Weaknesses

DEFINITION: Weaknesses, which are internal to the organization, are considered to be anything that the organization lacks, does not perform well, or a condition that hampers it in some way.

Please rate each weakness along a continuous scale where 5 = major weakness, 4 = less major weakness, 3 = average weakness, 2 = minor weakness, 1 = very minor weakness. Insert your rating in the blank column next to each weakness listed below.

Internal Weaknesses	Rating
No clear vision/objectives, thus leading to inefficiency.	

Source: Beekun, Rafik. *Strategic Planning and Implementation for Islamic Organizations.*
© Copyright: IIIT, 2006. All rights reserved.

APPENDIX-A

Worksheet #5
SWOT Analysis-Opportunities

DEFINITION: Opportunities originate from the EXTERNAL environment of the organization. They represent potential areas for growth, technological changes, demographic trends, etc.

Please rate each opportunity along a continuous scale where 5 = most attractive opportunity, 4 = attractive opportunity, 3 = average opportunity, 2 = less attractive opportunity, 1 = least attractive opportunity. Insert your rating in the blank column next to each opportunity listed below.

External Opportunities	Rating
Example: Establish a listserv for our members to share ideas and debate issues	

Source: Beekun, Rafik. *Strategic Planning and Implementation for Islamic Organizations.*
© Copyright: IIIT, 2006. All rights reserved.

Worksheet #6
SWOT Analysis-Threats
External Threats

DEFINITION: External threats pose a danger to the organization. Threats can emerge from the introduction of substitute technologies, the introduction of new/better services or products by competitors, new laws, or unfavorable demographic trends.

Rate each threat along a continuous scale where 5 = major threat, 4 = less major threat, 3 = average threat, 2 = minor threat, 1 = very minor threat. Insert your rating in the blank column next to each threat listed below.

External Threats	Rating
Example: Islamophobia is growing nationally and internationally	

Source: Beekun, Rafik. *Strategic Planning and Implementation for Islamic Organizations.*
© Copyright: IIIT, 2006. All rights reserved.

APPENDIX-A

Worksheet #7
Competitor Analysis

[This worksheet is partly adapted from McNamara, Carter. *Field Guide to Nonprofit Strategic Planning and Facilitation*. Minneapolis, Minnesota, 2003, pp. 254-255]

1. Name and location of competitor organization.

2. Rationale for considering it as a competitor (check all boxes that apply):
   ☐ Targets the same customer group or niche
   ☐ Provides the same or similar products or services
   ☐ Provides similar benefits
   ☐ Uses similar marketing and/or pricing strategy
   ☐ Uses similar distribution outlets or channels
   ☐ Uses similar financing strategy for customers
   ☐ Any other reason? Please list here.

3. What does our product or service offer that our competitor does not?

4. What does our product or service lack that our competitor provides?

5. Is there room for you and your competitor(s) in this niche or industry?

6. Do you wish to compete? If so, how? Note that Islam encourages competition, as long as it follows Islam's ethical principles. For more information, see the book *Islamic Business Ethics*.[1]

Source: Beekun, Rafik. *Strategic Planning and Implementation for Islamic Organizations.*
© Copyright: IIIT, 2006. All rights reserved.

Worksheet #8
Vision Statement

Write your vision statement (i.e., an idealized, future state that your organization is aiming towards). Please, remember that an organization's vision is broader than its mission statement and is very long-term oriented. It is typically short and concise.

- Will it inspire and galvanize your organization's members and external stakeholders? The words you use must inspire and motivate.

- Is it a short, positive, and vibrant statement?

- Can everyone memorize it?

Source: Beekun, Rafik. *Strategic Planning and Implementation for Islamic Organizations.*
© Copyright: IIIT, 2006. All rights reserved.

APPENDIX-A

Worksheet #9
Mission Statement

Write your mission statement. A mission statement can range from one sentence to several paragraphs; it states why the organization exists and what it hopes to accomplish now in order to achieve the organization's vision. Use an additional sheet of paper if necessary.

_____

- Does it explain the purpose or *raison d'être* of your organization?

- Does it describe to whom you are providing your services or products?

- Does it delineate how distinctive your service or product is and why your target customer group should want to deal with you instead of your competitor?

- Does it describe your geographical domain?
  (This may sometimes be necessary for a local or regional organization.)

Source: Beekun, Rafik. *Strategic Planning and Implementation for Islamic Organizations.*
© Copyright: IIIT, 2006. All rights reserved.

APPENDIX-A

Worksheet #10
Statement of Philosophy or Values

Write your values statement. Use additional sheets, if necessary:

```
_____
_____
_____
_____
_____
_____
```

- Does it reflect what is expected of your organization's participants when they act on the organization's behalf?

- Does it characterize how your organization wishes to be portrayed to both its internal and external stakeholders?

- Are these values congruent with an Islamic organizational culture?

Source: Beekun, Rafik. *Strategic Planning and Implementation for Islamic Organizations.*
© Copyright: IIIT, 2006. All rights reserved.

APPENDIX-A

Worksheet #11
Strategic Goals or Priorities

Fill out one worksheet for each strategic goal. State the goal:

_____

_____

_____

_____

Goal checklist:

- Does this goal fit our mission, vision, and/or statement of philosophy and values?

- Does it take into account our organizational strengths and opportunities, weaknesses and threats?

- What is its ranking in comparison to other strategic goals?

- Does it help us maximize value to our stakeholders?

Add additional stakeholders, as needed.

Stakeholder	Does it maximize value for this stakeholder? How?
Customers	
Employees	
Stockholders	
Community	

Source: Beekun, Rafik. *Strategic Planning and Implementation for Islamic Organizations.*
© Copyright: IIIT, 2006. All rights reserved.

Worksheet #12
Strategies

Fill out one worksheet for each strategy associated with a specific goal. Strategies describe how the mission and its associated goals will be achieved. State the strategy or strategies for each goal:

Goal:
Strategies:

Strategy checklist:

- ☐ Does this strategy fit our mission, vision, statement of philosophy and values, and goals?

- ☐ Does it take into account our organizational strengths and opportunities, weaknesses and threats?

- ☐ Does it fit in with other strategies being used for the same goal, or will it hamper their implementation?

- ☐ Does it fit in with the organization's overall strategy, or will it hamper its implementation?

Worksheet #13
Developing and Tracking an Operational or Action Plan [2]

Goal # _____ Goal Statement (*1 sentence*): _____

Strategies for this goal:
1.
2.
3.

Objectives for this goal using the above strategies:

Objective(s)	Action Steps Needed To Achieve Objective(s)	By Whom?	Starting Date / Ending Date	Resources Needed / Obtained From	Progress Date
1	1.1 1.2 1.3				
2	2.1 2.2 2.3				

Source: Beekun, Rafik. *Strategic Planning and Implementation for Islamic Organizations.*
© Copyright: IIIT, 2006. All rights reserved.

APPENDIX B

SAMPLE STRATEGIC PLANS AND CASE EXAMPLES

CASE #1
Global Foundation for People Living with WFS[1]
(A Fictitious Example)

A THREE-YEAR STRATEGIC PLAN: 2005 TO 2008

VISION: A permanent cure for WFS.

MISSION: To improve the quality of life for WFS sufferers by restoring and maintaining their dignity.

GOAL 1: To reduce the level of prejudice directed toward people affected by WFS in developing countries.

STRATEGY 1.1: Use the media effectively to reach the community-at-large.

LONG-TERM OBJECTIVE 1.1: Reduce prejudice against people living with WFS by the community-at-large by reaching 500,000 people with public service announcements within the next 2 years.

TARGET 1.1: Cooperate with NATION TV to develop and broadcast a multimedia campaign within the next 6 months on living a productive and positive life with WFS.

STRATEGY 1.2: Implement community activism programs for both in-school and out-of-school youth in Greater Qurazu.

LONG-TERM OBJECTIVE 1.2: Involve 3,000 14-17-year-olds in programs promoting humanitarian help and respect for WFS victims over the next 2 years.

TARGET 1.2: Establish a "Good Samaritan" program among 14-17-year-olds in Greater Qurazu within a year.

CASE #2
The Islamic Center of Long Island[2]
Website: www.1icli.com

'UNITY WITH DIVERSITY'

A HISTORY OF CHALLENGES

This community started out with only three people praying in the basement of a private house. Now, their community numbers at least 5,000 individuals. In addition, they have grown into one of the most dynamic Islamic centers in North America. Their center was completed by the grace of Allah, despite a lack of money and the surrounding community's initial opposition.

Challenges faced the center's founders before the construction even started. In February 1988, 90 of the neighboring residents in Westbury asked the town not to grant a building permit. Thanks to Allah, the mosque's leaders pursued their vision. For example, they invited their concerned neighbors to participate in the planning process and educated them about Islam. They participated in public meetings held by the town and maintained an ongoing dialogue with the Central Westbury Civic Association. Eventually, after concerns about parking congestion and other issues were allayed, the permission to build a 7,000 square-foot building without a minaret was granted in July 1989.

As construction was about to start, a new problem came up. A Muslim engineer agreed to supervise the construction, but the construction firm chosen to build the mosque was not Muslim. Again, the resulting concerns on the part of some Muslims were dealt with by seeking various fatwas for clarification.

During its construction, the center faced a financial crisis. Although the estimated costs were projected to be more than $1 million, $200,000 was available. Given that Islam prohibits dealing with interest, no interest-bearing loans could be sought from banks. As a result, the center was forced to build only what it could pay for and to raise funds from the Long Island Muslim community for the rest.

Another major hurdle occurred after obtaining a temporary certificate of occupancy and opening the facility for Friday prayers: The Westbury building inspector "closed" the facility due to "code" violations. However, she was so positively influenced by her interaction with the community that she embraced Islam and became one of the community's leading advocates. On February 8, 1998, the center's permanent certificate of occupancy was approved.

APPENDIX-B

After nine years of deliberation among brothers and sisters from the community and three years of construction, the Islamic Center of Long Island (ICLI) finally opened in time for Ramadan. It was the first mosque on Long Island built expressly to serve as a mosque, as opposed to being a building or home remodeled for that purpose. Final costs totaled about $2 million. Although most of the center's founders originally came from South Asia, it now has a very diverse group of attendees. Moreover, its architecture is designed to reflect this diversity.

INSTITUTIONALIZATION

ICLI was incorporated as a non-profit entity in April 1982 (Rajab 1402) under the provisions of the religious corporation law. Over a period of two to three years, the core founding group developed a set of rules and regulations. Since few members had any previous experience in mosque management, they decided to follow the Qur'an and the Sunnah in writing the center's by-laws. They also established an administrative structure to ensure its continued smooth operation. This combination of structure and by-laws served the growing community well during later unexpected and turbulent situations.

After the center was built, ICLI's members faced a major issue: What role it would play in Nassau, Long Island where more than one-half of its estimated 1.2 million inhabitants are Catholics and about one-fourth are Jewish, while Muslims were estimated to number no more than a few thousand. This exploration and definition of ICLI's *raison d'être* and future direction was dealt with in a systematic manner in April 2004: The center's leaders developed a strategic plan, parts of which have been used throughout this book. It is now described in detail.

VISION

To be a center of excellence for developing and sustaining a progressive, vibrant Islamic community and a nurturing environment for the society at large.

MISSION

To serve and engage Muslims by promoting the progressive values and teachings of Islam, and to advocate interfaith harmony in a multicultural environment in accordance with the Qur'an and Sunnah.

GOALS (in order of priority):

- Strengthen Islamic educational programs
- Focus on young adults
- Provide spiritual guidance and consultation
- Involve youth

- Project Islam in a positive manner through outreach activities
- Formalize infrastructure and the governance process
- Build a social support program
- Develop a sound financial base for ICLI.

After these goals were developed, several task forces were put together to outline explicit strategies and objectives for accomplishing them.

One Year Follow-up in 2005

In April 2005, ICLI assessed the progress made in implementing its strategic plan. Here is what its members had accomplished:

Goal 1: Strengthen Islamic Educational Programs – Chair: Sr. Laura.
- Establish a staff of qualified Sunday school teachers who would follow the curriclum. Status: Task completed with 16 qualified teachers and 3 qualified substitutes identified.
- Streamline and strengthen the ICLI education committee. Status: Task completed with regular updates and upgrades.

Goal 2: Focus on Young Adults – Chair: Sr. Honda.
- Provide preschool services. Status: Space renovation in progress. New York State application is pending, and start-up date is planned for early summer 2005.
- Young adult gatherings. Status: Two matrimonial dinners organized, and a mechanism and a methodology were put in place and are being refined.
- Mentoring programs. Status: No activity planned yet.

Goals 3 and 7: Provide Spiritual Guidance and Consultation, and Build a Social Support Program – Chair: Dr. Kaushal.
- Identify and train counselors. Status: No progress made yet.
- Identify professionals who can train volunteers. Status: Group has acquired deep expertise through the Domestic Harmony Committee over the past decade, but needs more volunteers.
- Advertise services via newsletter, Web, Friday and Sunday programs. Status: In process.

Goal 4: Involve Youth. Co-chairs: Br. Hamza and Sr. Reema
- Plan to link up with various Muslim Students' Association has not evolved as antipated. Status: Rethink this initiative.
- Big Brother/Big Sister program. Status: Rethink this initiative.
- Joint social action: blood drive/walkathon. Status: Rethink this initiative.

APPENDIX-B

Goal 5: Project Islam in a Positive Manner through Outreach Activities. Chair: Sr. Cathy
- Prepare appropriate material regarding Islam and Muslims. Status: A reference list of books has been compiled, and an outline of organized outreach activities is being shared.
- The revised updated website will be ready for launch by June 2005.
- A draft of the ICLI brochure has been prepared and circulated for suggestions.
- Plan open house at ICLI quarterly. Next one is set for May 2005.

Goal 6: Formalize Infrastructure and the Governance Process. Chair: Dr. Fakiuddin
- Task force recommendations have been presented to the ICLI board, which has approved most of them.
- A Governance and Grievance Committee has been established to address any concerns and/or conflicts among ICLI community members.

Goal 8: Develop a Sound Financial Base for ICLI. Chair: Dr. Nasir
- No progress report provided yet.

As mentioned earlier in this book, on average only about 30 percent of a strategic plan is implemented. Clearly, with the help of Allah, ICLI has surpassed the average in the very first year of implementing its systematic strategic plan. One must also note the sisters' tremendous contribution to the community, because they are involved in the centers' programs and activities. ICLI's sisters serve on the executive committee and the board of trustees – the center's highest policy- and decision-making bodies.

The remainder of this short case deals with a major ICLI strength and demonstrates how it has been harnessed effectively.

FOCUS ON GOAL #5 AND ITS IMPLEMENTATION
Interfaith and outreach activities have always been a distinctive core competency of ICLI's members. Several of their programs have earned the center a national reputation. This deep understanding of and working with other faith-based communities forms the foundation for goal #5 in ICLI's 2004 strategic plan.
- *Outreach to Members of Other Faiths.* In 1992, American Muslims and Jews in Dialogue (AMJID) was created with 15 members from each community. They met in each other's homes and began to learn about each other. Formed by Dr. Faroque Khan (current ICLI president) and Rabbi Jerome Davidson (Temple Beth-El's senior rabbi), AMJID has worked hard to break down the wall of ignorance separating the two faith communities. Large gatherings have taken place at the synagogue or the mosque for presentations on such topics

as "Understanding Judaism," "The Muslim American Community: Being a Minority in America," or "Jerusalem: City of Three Faiths." This deep mutual understanding was tremendously helpful after the 9/11 tragedy, when Muslims who had become the targets of hate and hysteria received words of support and encouragement from the Temple Beth-El community. In 2004, AMJID's activities were recognized with the Faith Fellowship Award, given by the Gathering of Light organization.

- *Outreach via Television.* In 2003, ICLI members helped Father Tom and Rabbi Gellman open up their television schedule for a 10-episode series on "Our Muslim Neighbors." Various topics have been covered, such as "Women in Islam," "Prophet Muhammad," "Hajj: The Muslim Pilgrimage," "Ramadan," and "The Holy Qur'an." This program was filmed by Telecare, a non-profit, state-of-the-art television and production facility belonging to the Diocese of Rockville Center. It reaches approximately 800,000 Catholics that are 33 years old or older. Telecare's programs are carried over another television channel that reaches an audience of 12 million people.

- *Outreach to Senior Citizens.* The Elderhostel Program is a not-for-profit organization that caters to 200,000 older adults each year, with over 10,000 programs in more than 90 countries and throughout the United States. After 9/11, the organization became concerned with "the proliferation of fear and confusion about Islam and Muslims throughout the US and the absence of easily identifiable resources for education about the Islamic faith."[3] As a result, Elderhostel formed a series of programs entitled "Building Bridges to Islam." In summer 2004, ICLI hosted 400 Elderhostel members to a lecture by Imam Feisal Abdul Rauf, author of *What's Right with Islam*. For a $59 Elderhostel fee, each participant received a copy of this book, an English-language translation of the Qur'an, an Islamic calendar, head scarves, and a Turkish takeout lunch. ICLI also created additional opportunities for Elderhostel members to learn about Islam and Muslims and for cultural exchange. Participants watched the Muslims pray *Dhuhr* prayer and listened to several presentations, including "Muslim Americans Post-9/11" and "Muslim Women." They also took part in a spirited question-and-answer session on "Myths and Misconceptions" surrounding Islam. Several families provided cultural and artistic artifacts and helped to put together an excellent cultural exhibit. This positive experience between ICLI and Elderhostel has led to a number of requests from other Elderhostel alumni groups who are interested in having their local Islamic centers provide speakers for their church and social groups. A repeat program at ICLI is planned for summer 2005.

- *First Annual Interfaith Iftar Dinner Celebration.* In 2005, ICLI, like many other Islamic centers in North America, hosted an interfaith Iftar dinner with their friends and neighbors as guests, including clergy from other faith-based communities, the police, the FBI, and local and state politicians. At least one of the guests fasted the entire month in solidarity with the Muslims. During the event, a short speech was given about fasting's physical and spiritual attributes.
- *Nassau Partnership for Healthy Communities* (NPHC). ICLI secured a grant that led to its being designated as one of the primary NPHC sites – a federally funded grant to help individuals in Nassau Country with no or poor access to health care. A joint effort with staff members from St. Francis Hospital was planned for 2005.
- *Tsunami Relief.* ICLI members donated generously toward the tsunami relief effort, and Islamically slaughtered (*qurbani*) meat was distributed in designated areas in Indonesia. At the same time, long-term assistance programs designed to support affected children and families with lost businesses are being developed. In addition, ICLI is partnering with a prominent Long Island organization, Family and Children's Services, in this long-term project.
- *Outreach to Sisters.* In March 2005, ICLI hosted a symposium on "Women and Access to Mosques." Three sisters led the discussion.
- *Outreach to "Reverts."* After the initial profession of faith (*shahadah*) and the ensuing hugs and greetings, what happens to these new Muslims is unclear. ICLI has worked hard to develop an ongoing educational and social forum for them.

Clearly, ICLI has faced a number of difficult issues over the years. Some of these are still being worked on, such as those dealing with family harmony, mental needs, and youth involvement. Nevertheless, ICLI is a center with heart and the right intention. By the grace of Allah, it has come a long way since 1982. Its first year track record with the strategic plan already shows that it has the will and discipline to achieve its vision and mission, Insha Allah.

APPENDIX C

Glossary of Islamic Terms[1]

`Adl	Justice, equilibrium, and equity. This fundamental value governs all social behavior and forms the basis of all social dealings and legal frameworks. Its opposite is *zulm* (injustice or inequity).
Akhirah	The Hereafter.
`Alayhi (`Alayha) al-Salam (*as*)	May Allah's peace be upon him (her).
Allah	The Creator and Sustainer of all that exists, the Supreme Being. This word is unique in that it has no root form or derivative forms.
Amanah	Something given to someone for safekeeping; a trust.
Amir	A leader.
`Asabiyyah	A concept according to which people put the needs of their family, group, or clan ahead of the community's needs; a core social value of the pre-Islamic Arabs.
Awqaf	A religious foundation set up with charitable donations in order to provide a specific benefit to the community.
Ayat	A section of the text of the Qur'an referred to as a "verse." It literally means a sign, indication or message.
`Azm	Resolve.
Bay`ah	Pledging one's allegiance to a specific person.
Caliph	The leader of the Muslim Ummah.
Da`wah	Invitation; call. Refers to the duty of Muslims to invite or call others (both Muslims and non-Muslims) to the straight and natural path of Islam or submission to Allah.
Deen	Religion; a way of life. It is most commonly used to refer to Islam and the way of life that it ordains.
Du`a	A supplication or personal prayer made to Allah; invocation.

APPENDIX-C

Dunya	The present world in which we live, as opposed to the Hereafter.
Fi Sabil Allah	In the way of Allah; for Allah's cause.
Hadith	Literally an account. It is most commonly used in the context of the many narrations and reports of the Prophet's actions and sayings.
Halal	Anything that is permitted by the Shari`ah (Islamic law).
Haram	Anything that is prohibited by the Shari`ah (Islamic law).
Hijrah	The Prophet's migration from Makkah to Madinah; to leave one's place of residence either for His sake or some other reason; leaving a bad practice in order to adopt a righteous way of life. The Islamic calendar begins in 622, the year in which this event occurred.
Ihsan	Literally to do good or excel. One of the highest degrees of *iman* (faith) where one serves Allah as if one is seeing Him, and if one cannot see Him, then He definitely sees His servant. *Ihsan* also means benevolence.
Imam	A person who leads any of the five prescribed prayers; a leader (in general), a reputable scholar, or the leader of a Muslim country.
Iman	Faith in the articles of faith enunciated in the Qur'an and the Sunnah.
Insha' Allah	God willing.
Islam	To submit to Allah and offer peace; the religion followed by all Muslims.
Istikhara	Salat al-istikhara is a special prayer for divine guidance concerning a difficult problem or for choosing the correct option.
Jahiliyyah	The pre-Islamic status quo known among Muslims as the "Age of Ignorance (of Islam)" immediately before Allah chose Muhammad as His messenger to the Arabs.
Jihad	Literally to struggle. "Any earnest striving in the way of Allah, involving either personal effort, material resources, or arms for righteousness and against evil, wrongdoing, and oppression. Where it involves armed struggle, it must be for the defense of the Muslim community or a just war to protect even non-Muslims from evil, oppression, and tyranny."

APPENDIX-C

Khalifah	Steward, vicegerent, successor. Man is referred to in the Qur'an (*Surat Al Baqara,* 2:30) as the *khalifah* or steward of Allah on earth. "The word *khalifah* was used after the death of the Prophet Muhammad (p) to refer to his successor, Abu Bakr (ra), as head of the Muslim community. Later, it came to be accepted as the designation for the head of the Muslim state. Anglicized as Caliph."
Madinah / Yathrib	A city in present-day Saudi Arabia where Prophet Muhammad is buried; the city of the Prophet.
Makkah	A city in present-day Saudi Arabia where the Ka'bah is located.
Masjid	A place of worship for Muslims.
Muslim	One who believes in the one God (Allah) and Prophet Muhammad; one who submits to Allah's will.
Nasihah	Advice.
Niyyah	Intention.
Qur'an	Allah's final revelation to humanity; revealed to the Prophet over 23 years.
Qurbani	The ritual sacrifice of a cow, goat or sheep. This practice originated with Prophet Abraham, who was willing to sacrifice his son Isma`il (Ishmael) in obedience to Allah's command. This was the ultimate test of Prophet Abraham's faith, and he passed it successfully. The ritual sacrifice of an animal is now obligatory (*wajib*) on those Muslims who have acquired a certain amount of wealth.
(ra)	*Radi Allahu `anhu (masculine) or Radi Allahu `anha (feminine).* May Allah be pleased with him or her.
Rasul Allah	Messenger of Allah (Prophet Muhammad).
(saw)	*Salla Allahu `alayhi wa Sallam.* Abbreviated words of honor and salutations attached to the name of the Holy Prophet Muhammad. May Allah send blessings and salutations on him.
Sahih	Literally, sound. When used in reference to a hadith, it means a hadith whose chain of narrators is authentic in belief, character, and memory.

APPENDIX-C

Sirah	Lit., conduct. The study of the life of the Prophet.
Shari`ah	Literally a path. the legal system of Islam.
Shura	The consultative process of decision making.
Sunnah	Literally, a tradition or practice; the collection of the Prophet's traditions, practices, words, actions, and what has been allowed/prohibited by him.
Tafseer or Tafsir	Commentary or exegesis; the science of explaining and commenting on the Qur'an's verses.
Taqwa	Piety: fear, consciousness of, and respect/awe for Allah.
Tarbiyyah	Training toward self-development; education.
Tawhid	Allah's absolute Oneness.
Tayammum	Ablution made with dust in the absence of water.
Ummah	The global community of Muslims, irrespective of color, race, language, nationality, or borders; the universal body of Muslims as a single community.
Wudhu'	An ablution with water that must be performed before the prescribed prayer.
Yathrib	See Madinah
Zakah	The amount payable by a Muslim on his net worth as a part of his religious obligation, mainly for the benefit of the poor and the needy.

ENDNOTES

Quotable Quotes

1. The Arabic term 'Allah' is the proper noun for God. It refers to the One and Only Creator, Sustainer, and Cherisher of the Universe. From the Muslim perspective, the term 'Allah' is preferable to the term 'God', not only because it is the proper name of God, but also because the term 'Allah' is not subject to gender or plurality (Badawi, 2001). The term 'Allah' will be used in this book.
2. (p) refers to and means abbreviated words of honor and salutations attached to the name of Prophet Muhammad (p). These words mean: may Allah send blessings and salutations on him. This particular quote comes from Yusuf al-Qaradawi, *Dawr al-Qiyam wa al-Akhlaq fi al-Iqtisad al-Islami* (Maktabat Wahbah:1995).
3. As cited in R. H. Migliore, R. E. Stevens, D. L. Loudon, and S. Williamson, *Strategic Planning for Not-for-Profit Organizations* (Binghamton, NY: The Haworth Press, 1995).
4. (ra) May Allah be pleased with him or her.
5. *Salla Allahi `Alaihi wa al-Salam*. Abbreviated words of honor and salutations attached to the name of the Holy Prophet Muhammad. These words mean: may Allah send blessings and salutations on him.
6. As cited in Hisham Altalib, *Training Guide for Islamic Workers* (Herndon, VA: International Institute of Islamic Thought, 1991).

Chapter 1

1. The Qur'an is the holy book of Muslims revealed by Allah to Muhammad (p). When we refer to selected *surahs* (chapters) and *ayats* (verses) in it, we will use the convention xx:yy where xx will refer to the Qur'anic chapter and yy will refer to the Qur'anic verse within that chapter. The following translation of the Qur'an was used: *The Holy Qur'an: Text,*
2. *Translation and Commentary*, tr. Abdullah Yusuf Ali (Beltsville, MD: Amana publications, 1989).
3. M. Marshall, 'Is Strategic Planning Biblical? Looking at Leaders from Scripture', *Church Administration* (Fall 2002).
4. (as) is an abbreviation of 'peace be upon him', an honorific formula that Muslims use when
5. the name of a prophet – other than Muhammad (p) – is mentioned.
6. Altalib, *Training Guide.*
7. A. Kutty, 'Fatwa,' (Online at: www.Islamonline.net, 2002.)
8. S. A. Rosly, 'The Inseparable *Shar`i* and *Tab`i* Principles in Business Strategy', (Online at: www.dinarstandard.com, 2004.)
9. Ibid.
10. Ibid.

ENDNOTES

11. Altalib, *Training Guide.*
12. L. D. Goodstein, T. M. Nolan, and J. W. Pfeiffer, *Applied Strategic Planning: An Overview* (San Diego: Pfeiffer and Company, 1992).
13. J. M. Bryson, *Strategic Planning for Public and Nonprofit Organizations* (San Francisco: Jossey-Bass, 1995), p. 5.
14. *Quotations by General George Patton.* (Online at www.generalpatton.com.)
15. A. H. Siddiqui, *Sahih Muslim* volume 3, (n.p.: n.d.), hadith 4810, p. 1078.
16. R. Wiggins and T. Ruefli, 'Sustained Competitive Advantage:Temporal Dynamics and the Incidence and Persistence of Superior Economic Performance,' *Organization Science* 13(1) (2002): pp. 82-107.
17. G. Hawawini, V. Subramanian, and P. Verdin, 'Is Performance Driven by Industry or Firm-specific Factors? A New Look at the Evidence,' *Strategic Management Journal* 24(1) (2003), pp. 1-16.
18. J. Collins, *From Good to Great* (San Francisco: Jossey-Bass, 2003).
19. Goodstein, Nolan, and Pfeiffer, *Applied Strategic Planning.*
20. M. Lings, *Muhammad: His Life Based on the Earliest Sources* (Rochester, VT: Inner Traditions, 1983).
21. Based on work done by Beekun, R., Carslaw, C. and Stedham, Y., (1997).
22. R. M. Grant, *Contemporary Strategy Analysis* (Oxford, UK: Blackwell, 2004).
23. N. Jabnoun, *Islam and Management* (Riyadh: International Islamic Publishing House, 2001).

Chapter 2
1. Ibn Taymiyyah, *Al-Siyasat al-Shari`ah fi Islah al-Ra'i wa al-Ra'iyyha* (On Public and Private Law in Islam) (Beirut: Khayats, 1966).
2. R. Beekun, 'Assessing the Effectiveness of Socio-technical Interventions: Antidote or Fad?' *Human Relations* 42(10) (1989) pp. 877-97.
3. G. Hofstede, *Culture's Consequences: International Differences in Work-Related Values* (Thousand Oaks, CA: Sage Publications, 2001).
4. I. Janis, *Victims of Groupthink: A Psychological Study of Foreign Policy Decisions and Fiascos* (Boston: Houghton Mifflin, 1973).
5. E. R. Freeman, *Strategic Management: A Stakeholder Approach* (Boston: Pitman, 1984); R. Phillips, *Stakeholder Theory and Organizational Ethics* (San Francisco: Berrett-Koehler, 2003).
6. A. Bedeian and R. Zammuto, *Organizations: Theory and Design* (New York: Dryden, 1991).
7. *Sirah Ibn Hisham* (n.p.: n.d.), vol. 2, p. 282. Cited in A. I. Akram, 'Khalid bin Al-Waleed: The Sword of Allah,' (1969). Online at www.swordofallah.com.
8. Institute for Social Policy and Understanding, 'Enhancing Board Performance in the Islamic Nonprofit Sector', (2005). *Online* at www.ispu.us.

9. E. A. Lawler, D. L. Finegold, G. S. Benson, and J. A. Conger, 'Corporate Boards: Keys to Effectiveness', *Organizational Dynamics* 30(4) (2002), pp. 310-24.
10. Ibid.
11. J. A. Pearce and S. A. Zahra, 'The Relative Power of CEOs and Boards of Directors: Associations with Corporate Performance,' *Strategic Management Journal* 12(2) (1991), pp. 135-53.

Chapter 3

1. R. Beekun and J. Badawi, *Leadership: An Islamic Perspective* (Brentwood, MD: amana publications, 1999).
2. A. W. Hamid, *Companions of the Prophet* (Leicester, UK: MELS, 1995), vol. 2, pp. 28-29.
3. D. F. Spulber, *Management Strategy* (Burr Ridge, IL: McGraw-Hill/Irwin, 2004).
4. Thompson, Jr., Gamble, and Strickland, *Strategy*.
5. J. B. Barney and W. S. Hesterly, *Strategic Management and Competitive Advantage: Concepts and Cases* (Upper Saddle River, NJ: Prentice-Hall, 2005).
6. G. Hamel and C. K. Prahalad, *Competing for the Future* (Cambridge, MA: Harvard Business School Press, 1994).
7. Collins, *From Good to Great*.
8. Barney and Hesterly, *Strategic Management*.
9. J. Abrahams, *The Mission Statement Book* (Berkeley: Ten Speed Press, 1995).
10. E. H. Schein, *Organizational Culture and Leadership*, 2nd edn, (San Francisco: Jossey-Bass, 1997).
11. Spulber, *Management Strategy*.
12. Barney and Hesterly, *Strategic Management*.
13. Spulber, *Management Strategy*.
14. Janis, *Victims of Groupthink*.
15. P. Kotler, *Marketing Management: Analysis, Planning and Control* (Upper Saddle River, NJ: Prentice-Hall, 2005).
16. A. I. Akram, 'Khalid bin Al-Waleed.'
17. M. E. Porter, *Competitive Advantage* (New York: Free Press, 1995).
18. H. Mintzberg, *Structure in Fives: Designing Effective Organizations* (Upper Saddle River, NJ: Prentice-Hall, 1983).
19. Thompson, Jr., Gamble, and Strickland, *Strategy*.

Chapter 4

1. B. George, *Authentic Leadership* (San Francisco, CA: Jossey-Bass, 2003).
2. Lings, *Muhammad*, p. 218.
3. J. C. Fisher and K. M. Cole, *Leadership and Management of Volunteer Programs* (San Francisco, CA: Jossey-Bass, 1993).

ENDNOTES

4. Thompson, Jr., Gamble, and Strickland, *Strategy*.
5. www.americanrhetoric.com/speeches/Ihaveadream.htm.
6. O. A. El Sawy, 'Temporal Perspectives and Managerial Attention: A Study of Chief Executive Strategic Behavior', (Ph.D. dissertation, Stanford University, 1983); J. M. Kouzes and B. Z. Posner, *The Leadership Challenge* (San Francisco, CA: Jossey-Bass, 1995).
7. Kouzes and Posner, *The Leadership Challenge*.
8. W. Bennis, *On Becoming a Leader* (Reading, MA: Addison-Wesley, 1989).
9. Kouzes and Posner, *The Leadership Challenge*.
10. Janis, *Victims of Groupthink*.
11. A. A. Behzadnia and S. Denny, *To the Commander in Chief from Imam Ali to Malik-E-Ashter* (n.p.: n.d.).
12. Collins, *From Good to Great*.
13. Abrahams, *The Mission Statement Book*, p. 40.
14. S. R. Covey, *The Seven Habits of Highly Effective People* (New York: Fireside, 1989), p. 143
15. Jabnoun, *Islam and Management*.
16. Thompson, Jr., Gamble, and Strickland, *Strategy*.
17. George, *Authentic Leadership*.
18. D. F. Abell, *Defining the Business: The Starting Point of Strategic Planning* (Englewood Cliffs, NJ: Prentice Hall, 1980).
19. T. Peters and R. Waterman *In Search of Excellence* (New York, NY: Harper & Row, 1982).
20. T. Levitt, 'Marketing Myopia', *Harvard Business Review* (July-August 1960), pp. 45-56.
21. Ibid.
22. M. E. Porter, *Competitive Advantage* (New York, NY: Free Press, 1995).
23. www.ameenhousing.com.
24. Thompson, Jr., Gamble, and Strickland, *Strategy*.

Chapter 5
1. Narrated by Aisha (*raa*) in *Sahih al-Bukhari* (n.p.: n.d.), hadith no. 4.760
2. Spulber, *Management Strategy*.
3. J. March and H. Simon, *Organizations* (New York, NY: Wiley, 1958).

Chapter 6
none

Chapter 7
1. James Brian Quinn, *Strategies for Change: Logical Incrementalism* (Homewood, IL: Irwin, 1980).
2. Collins, *From Good to Great*.

ENDNOTES

3. W. Khan, *Muhammad: A Prophet for Humanity* (New Delhi, India: Goodword Books, 1998).
4. Spulber, *Management Strategy*.
5. M. Saeed, Z. U. Ahmed, and S. Mukhtar, 'International Marketing Ethics from an Islamic Perspective: A Value-maximization Approach', *Journal of Business Ethics* 32 (2001), pp. 127-42.
6. Rafik I. Beekun, *Islamic Business Ethics* (Herndon, VA: International Institute of Islamic Thought, 1997).
7. A. Marcus, *Management Strategy: Sustaining Competitive Advantage* (Burr Ridge, Il: McGraw Hill/Irwin, 2005).
8. Thompson, Jr., Gamble, and Strickland, *Strategy*.

Chapter 8
1. Kouzes and Posner, *The Leadership Challenge*.
2. Migliore, Stevens, Loudon, and Williamson, *Strategic Planning*.

Chapter 9
1. A. I. Akram, 'Khalid bin Al-Waleed.'
2. Beekun and Badawi, *Leadership*.
3. Jabnoun, *Islam and Management*.
4. G. L. Morrisey, *A Guide to Tactical Planning* (San Francisco: Jossey-Bass, 1996).
5. Beekun and Badawi, *Leadership*.

Chapter 10
1. *Fiqh al-Sunnah*, 4.1. in *Winalim* (1996). (Silver Springs, MD: ISL Software Corporation, Release 4).
2. A. I. Akram, 'Khalid bin Al-Waleed.'
3. Morrisey, *A Guide to Tactical Planning*.
4. Porter, *Competitive Advantage*.
5. Lings, *Muhammad*.
6. Ibid.
7. P. Schwartz, *The Art of the Long View* (New York: Doubleday, 1997).
8. Thompson, Jr., Gamble, and Strickland, *Strategy*.
9. G. Ringland, *Scenarios in Business* (West Sussex, UK: Wiley, 2002).

Chapter 11
1. L. Gerstner, Jr., *Who Says Elephants Can't Dance? Leading A Great Enterprise Through Dramatic Change* (New York, NY: Harper Business, 2003).

ENDNOTES

2. Beekun and Badawi, *Leadership*.
3. J. C. Rost, *Leadership for the Twenty-First Century* (New York: Praeger, 1991).
4. J. M. Burns, *Leadership* (New York, NY: Harper & Row, 1978), p. 19
5. Ibid.
6. Al-Azdi, *Sunan Abu Dawud*, in *Winalim* (1996). (Silver Springs, MD: ISL Software Corporation, Release 4).
7. Imam Ali, *Al-Bukhari,* hadith 5.629, in *Winalim* (1996). (Silver Springs, MD: ISL Software Corporation, Release 4).
8. Collins, *Good to Great.*
9. Kouzes and Posner, *The Leadership Challenge.*
10. *Al-Tirmidhi* and *Ibn Majah*, in *Winalim* (1996). (Silver Springs, MD: ISL Software Corporation, Release 4.)
11. *Al-Bukhari*. In Winalim (1996). (Silver Springs, MD: ISL Software Corporation, Release 4.)
12. Kouzes and Posner, *The Leadership Challenge.*
13. J. P. Kotter, *A Force for Change: How Leadership Differs from Management* (New York: Free Press, 1990).
14. R. Greenleaf, *The Servant as Leader* (Indianapolis: Greenleaf Center for Servant-Leadership, 1970).
15. *Al-Tirmidhi*, in *Winalim* (1996). (Silver Springs, MD: ISL Software Corporation, Release 4.)
16. http://www.amaana.org
17. Kouzes and Posner, *The Leadership Challenge.*
18. L. G. Bolman and T. E. Deal, *Reframing Organizations: Artistry, Choice, and Leadership* (San Francisco: Jossey Bass, 1997).
19. Kouzes and Posner, *The Leadership Challenge.*
20. M. Bazerman, R. Beekun, and D. Schoorman, 'Performance Evaluation in a Dynamic Context: A Laboratory Study of the Impact of a Prior Commitment to the Ratee,' *Journal of Applied Psychology* 67 (1982), pp. 873-76.
21. Kouzes and Posner, *The Leadership Challenge.*
22. Al-Tirmidhi, in *Winalim* (1996). (Silver Springs, MD: ISL Software Corporation, Release 4.)
23. K. Weick, *The Social Psychology of Organizing* (Reading, MA: Addison Wesley, 1979).

Chapter 12
1. *The Bible* (New King James Version) (Nashville, TN: Thomas Nelson Publishers, 1982).
2. Mintzberg, *Structure in Fives.*
3. J. Gibson, J. Ivancevich, and J. Donnelly, *Organizations: Behavior, Structure, and Processes* (Burr Ridge, IL: Irwin-McGraw Hill, 2001).
4. Daft, *Organization Theory*
5. R. Daft, *Organization Theory and Design* (St. Paul, MN: West Publishing, 1989).

6. T. Burns and G. M. Stalker, *Management of Innovation* (London: Tavistock Publications,1961).
7. Porter, *Competitive Advantage*.
8. Daft, *Organization Theory*.
9. Bedeian and Zammuto, *Organizations*.
10. R. Duncan, 'What is the right organization structure?,' *Organization dynamics*, Winter 59-79, 1979.
11. Mintzberg, *Structure in Fives*.
12. Daft, *Organization Theory*.
13. Daft, *Organization Theory*

Chapter 13
1. Schein, *Organizational Culture*, 10.
2. Gibson, Ivancevich, and Donnelly, *Organizations*.
3. Abu Hurayrah, *Sahih al-Bukhari*, in *Winalim* (1996). (Silver Springs, MD: ISL Software Corporation, Release 4.)
4. R. Covington, 'Humanitarian to a Nation,' *Saudi Aramco World* (Nov/Dec: 2004), p. 33.
5. Anas ibn Malik, *Sunan Abu Dawud* (hadith no. 1637), in *Winalim* (1996). (Silver Springs, MD: ISL Software Corporation, Release 4.)
6. Covington, 'Humanitarian'; www.paks.net/edhi-foundation.
7. Schein, *Organizational Culture*.
8. H. Kelleher, *Nuts! Southwest Airlines' Crazy Recipe for Business and Personal Success* (Austin, TX: Bard Press, 1996).
9. Beekun and Badawi, *Leadership*.
10. A. Siddiqui, 'Ethics in Islam: Key Concepts and Contemporary Challenges', *Journal of Moral Education* 26(4) (1997), pp. 423-32.
11. I. R. Al-Faruqi, *Al Tawhid: Its Implications for Thought and Life* (Herndon, VA: IIIT, 1992).
12. M. Ahmad, *Business Ethics in Islam* (Islamabad, IIIT, 1995).
13. Beekun, *Islamic Business Ethics*.
14. R. Beekun and J. Badawi, 'Balancing Ethical Responsibility among Multiple Stakeholders: The Islamic Perspective', *Journal of Business Ethics* 60 (2005) pp: 131-45.
15. J. Collins and J. Porras, *Built to Last: Successful Habits of Visionary Companies* (New York: Harper Business, 1999).
16. Collins, *From Good to Great*.
17. Rafi-uddin Shikoh, 'Savola Group's Balanced Way: A Sure Ingredient for Sustained Growth'. Online at www.dinarstandard.com, Oct 1, 2004. Reprinted with permission.
18. http://www.savola.com.
19. Ibid.
20. Ibid.
21. Collins, *From Good to Great*.
22. Burns, *Leadership*.

ENDNOTES

Chapter 14
1. Migliore, Stevens, Loudon, and Williamson, *Strategic Planning*.
2. Y. al-Qaradawi, *Dawr al-Qiyam wa al-Akhlaq fi al-Iqtisad al-Islami* (Maktabat Wahbah: 1995).
3. General Accounting Office/General Government Division, GAO/GCD-10.1.20. *The Results Act: An Evaluator's Guide to Assessing Agency Annual Performance Plans* (April 1998, version 1).
4. Savola Group, 'Winning in the MENA Region and Beyond'. Online at www.savola.com.
5. Migliore, Stevens, Loudon, and Williamson, *Strategic Planning*.
6. General Accounting Office/General Government Division, GAO/GCD-10.1.20. *The Results Act*.
7. Ibid.
8. Ibid.
9. Ibid.
10. Altalib, *Training Guide*.

Chapter 15
1. Collins, *From Good to Great*.

Chapter 16
1. George, *Authentic Leadership*, p. 5.
2. Abu Hurayrah, in *Abu Dawud*.
3. Beekun and Badawi, 'Balancing Ethical Responsibility.'
4. *Sahih al-Bukhari*, hadith no. 1.1., in *Winalim*.
5. Y. al-Qaradawi, *Al-Halal wa al-Haram fi al-Islam* (Indianapolis: American Trust Publications, n.d.).
6. An-Nawawi, *Hadith Qudsi* (Beirut, Lebanon: The Holy Qur'an Publishing House, 1979), hadith no. 37.
7. Al Qaradawi, *Al-Halal wa al-Haram*, p. 32. Please note that necessity does dictate exceptions and Islam is aware of the crises and emergencies that one may face. As seen in Qur'an 2:173, Allah allows Muslims to eat *haram* food (e.g., pork, blood, dead animals) if they are faced with certain starvation. Under such duress, Muslims need not embrace the haram eagerly and should return to the *halal* as soon as possible. See al-Qaradawi, *Al-Halal wa al-Haram*, 36-38.
8. Beekun, *Islamic Business Ethics*.
9. Beekun and Badawi, *Leadership*.
10. Beekun and Badawi, 'Balancing Ethical Responsibility.'
11. Freeman, *Strategic Management*.

12. Ibid.
13. Beekun and Badawi, 'Balancing Ethical Responsibility.'
14. Siddiqui, 2002.
15. Beekun, *Islamic Business Ethics*.
16. Ahmad, *Business Ethics in Islam*.
17. Muhammad 'Umar-ud-din, *The Ethical Philosophy of Al-Ghazzali* (Sh. Muhammad Ashraf, Lahore, Pakistan, 1991), p. 241.
18. Iyad Ibn Himar, *Sahih Muslim*, hadith no. 6853, Winalim, (1996). (Silver Springs, MD: ISL Software Corporation, Release 4.)
19. Siddiqui, 'Ethics in Islam', pp. 423-32.
20. Beekun and Badawi, 'Balancing Ethical Responsibility'; Freeman, *Strategic Management*; E. R. Freeman, 'A Stakeholder Theory of the Modern Corporation', in T. L. Beauchamp and N. E. Bowie, eds., *Ethical Theory and Business* (Upper Saddle River, NJ: Prentice-Hall, 2001), pp. 56-65.
21. S. Qutb, *Social Justice in Islam* (New York: Octagon Books, 1980), p. 56.
22. T. L. Beauchamp and N. E. Bowie, *Ethical Theory and Business*, 7th edn (Upper Saddle River, NJ: Prentice-Hall, 2004).
23. Ibid
24. *Sahih al-Bukhari*, hadith no. 7.128, in *Winalim*.
25. *Sahih Muslim*, hadith no. 4491, in *Winalim*.

Chapter 17
1. Reported by Talq b. Habib, *Fiqh-us-Sunnah*, 4.115, in Winalim.
2. *Sahih al-Bukhari*, hadith no. 4.584, in *Winalim*.
3. Jabnoun, I*slam and Management*.
4. Online at: www.java-man.com/Pages/JamiAlUloom/hadith_49.html; www.islaam.com/Article.aspx?id=432.
5. Abdul Malik Mujahid, 'Tawakkul.' Reprinted with permission from www.soundvision.com.
6. Qatadah, *Fiqh as-Sunnah*, 4.141, in Winalim
7. Loc. cit.

Final Words
1. M. Iqbal, *Khizr-E-Raah*, tr. Tariq and Aziz (Lahore: Pan Islamic Publications, n.d.)

Appendix A
1. Beekun, *Islamic Business Ethics*.
2. Adapted from material developed by the Western Region Campus Compact Consortium members, 2000-01.

ENDNOTES

Appendix B
1. This fictitious case example was modeled after the case example on the website of AIDSMAP located at: http://www.aidsmap.com
2. Material for this case was generously provided by Dr. Faroque Khan, current president and one of the founders of ICLI. Other sources included material excepted from the ICLI website at www.1icli.com and from articles published about ICLI in the *New York Times*: " A First Mosque," (Dec. 18, 1988), and "L.I. Mosque Is Sign of Islam's Community Growth: A New House of Worship Fills Both a Social and a Religious Void," (February 25, 1993).
3. Letter from James Moses, president/CEO of Elderhostel to Dr. Khan and ICLI.

Appendix C
1. Based on an integration of definitions from glossaries in Islamic Scholar Software, *Taqwa: The Provision of Believers* (London: Al Firdous, 1996), and Dr. Taha Jabir Al-Alwani, *Ethics of Disagreement in Islam* (Herndon, VA: International Institute of Islamic Thought, 1994).

BIBLIOGRAPHY

Abell, D. F., *Defining the Business: The Starting Point of Strategic Planning*. Englewood Cliffs, NJ: Prentice Hall, 1980.

Abrahams, J. *The Mission Statement Book*. Berkeley, CA: Ten Speed Press, 1995.

Ahmad, M., *Business Ethics in Islam*. Islamabad: International Institute of Islamic Thought, 1995.

Akram, A. I., *Khalid bin Al-Waleed: The Sword of Allah*. Online at www.swordofallah.com, 1969.

Al Alwani, Taha Jabir, *Ethics of Disagreement in Islam*. Herndon, VA: International Institute of Islamic Thought, 1994.

Ali, Abdullah Yusuf, *The Holy Qur'an: Text, Translation and Commentary*. Beltsville, MD: amana publications, 2004.

Altalib, Hisham, *Training Guide for Islamic Workers*. Herndon, VA: International Institute of Islamic Thought, 1991.

Badawi, G., *Islamic Business Ethics*. Indianapolis, IN: International Business Trade Forum, 2001.

Barney, J. B. and Hesterly, W. S., *Strategic Management and Competitive Advantage: Concepts and Cases*. Upper Saddle River, NJ: Prentice-Hall, 2005.

Bazerman, M., Beekun, R. and Schoorman, D., 'Performance Evaluation in a Dynamic Context: A Laboratory Study of the Impact of a Prior Commitment to the Ratee', *Journal of Applied Psychology*, 67 (1982), pp. 873-76.

Beauchamp, T. L. and Bowie, N. E., *Ethical Theory and Business*, 7th edn. Upper Saddle River, NJ: Prentice-Hall, 2004.

Bedeian, A. and Zammuto, R., *Organizations: Theory and Design*. New York, NY: Dryden, 1991.

Beekun, R., 'Assessing the Effectiveness of Socio-technical Interventions: Antidote or Fad?', *Human Relations*, 42(10) (1989), pp. 877-897.

Beekun, Rafik I., *Islamic Business Ethics*. Herndon, VA: International Institute of Islamic Thought, 1997.

Beekun, R. and Badawi, J., *Leadership: An Islamic Perspective*. Brentwood, MD: amana-publications, 1999.

Beekun, R. and Badawi, J., 'Balancing Ethical Responsibility among Multiple Stakeholders: The Islamic Perspective', *Journal of Business Ethics*, 60 (2005), pp. 131-45.

Behzadnia, A. A. and Denny, S., *To the Commander in Chief from Imam Ali to Malik-E-Ashter* (n.p.: n.d.).

Bennis, W., 'The Four Competencies of Leadership,' *National Forum* 71(1) (Winter 1991), pp. 12-15.

BIBLIOGRAPHY

Bible. New King James Version. Nashville, TN: Thomas Nelson Publishers, 1982.

Bolman, L. G. and Deal, T. E., *Reframing Organizations: Artistry, Choice, and Leadership.* San Francisco, CA: Jossey Bass, 1997.

Bryson, J. M., *Strategic Planning for Public and Nonprofit Organizations.* San Francisco, CA: Jossey-Bass, 1995.

Burns, J. M., *Leadership.* New York, NY: Harper & Row, 1978.

Burns, Tom and Stalker, G. M. *Management of Innovation*, London, Tavistock Publications, 1961.

Collins, J., *From Good to Great.* San Francisco, CA: Jossey-Bass, 2003.

Collins, J., and Porras, J., *Built to Last: Successful Habits of Visionary Companies.* New York, NY: Harper Business, 1999.

Conger, J. A., 'The Dark Side of Leadership', *Organizational Dynamics* (Autumn 1990), pp. 44-55.

Covey, S. R., *The Seven Habits of Highly Effective People.* New York, NY: Fireside, 1989.

Covington, R., 'Humanitarian to a Nation', *Saudi Aramco World*, (November/December 2004), pp. 33-43.

Daft, R. *Organization Theory and Design.* St. Paul, MN: West Publishing, 1989.

Digman, L., *Strategic Management: Concepts, Decisions and Cases.* Homewood, IL: BPI/Irwin, 1990.

Duncan, R., "What is the right organization structure?", *Organization dynamics* (Winter 1979), pp. 59-79

El Sawy, O. A., 'Temporal Perspectives and Managerial Attention: A Study of Chief Executive Strategic Behavior', (Unpublished Ph.D. dissertation, Stanford University, 1983).

Al-Faruqi, I. R., *Al Tawhid: Its Implications for Thought and Life.* Herndon, VA: International Institute of Islamic Thought, 1992.

Fisher, J. C. and Cole, K. M., *Leadership and Management of Volunteer Programs.* San Francisco, CA: Jossey-Bass, 1993.

Freeman, E. R., *Strategic Management: A Stakeholder Approach.* Boston, MA: Pitman, 1984.

Freeman, E. R., 'A Stakeholder Theory of the Modern Corporation.' In Beauchamp, T. L. and N. E. Bowie, eds., *Ethical Theory and Business.* Upper Saddle River, NJ: Prentice-Hall, (2001), pp. 56-65.

General Accounting Office/General Government Division, GAO/GCD-10.1.20. *The Results Act: An Evaluator's Guide to Assessing Agency Annual Performance Plans, April, 1998.* Version 1.

Gerstner, L. Jr., *Who Says Elephants Can't Dance? Leading a Great Enterprise through Dramatic Change.* New York, NY: Harper Business, 2003.

Gibson, J., Ivancevich, J. and Donnelly, J., *Organizations: Behavior, Structure and Processes.* Burr Ridge, IL: Irwin-McGraw Hill, 2001.

BIBLIOGRAPHY

Goodstein, L. D., Nolan, T. M., and Pfeiffer, J. W., *Applied Strategic Planning: An Overview,* San Diego, CA: Pfeiffer and Company, 1992.

Greenleaf, R., *The Servant as Leader.* Indianapolis, IN: Greenleaf Center for Servant-Leadership, 1970.

George, B., *Authentic Leadership.* San Francisco, CA: Jossey-Bass, 2003.

Goodstein, L. D, Nolan, T. M. and Pfeiffer, J. W., *Applied Strategic Planning: An Overview.* San Diego, CA: Pfeiffer and Company, 1992.

Grant, R. M., *Contemporary Strategy Analysis.* Oxford, UK: Blackwell, 2004.

Hamel, G. and Prahalad, C. K., *Competing for the Future.* Cambridge, MA: Harvard Business School Press, 1994.

Hamid, Abul Wahid, *Companions of the Prophet.* Leicester, UK: MELS, Volume 2, pp. 28-29, 1995.

Harrison, R., and Stokes, H., *Diagnosing Organizational Culture.* San Diego, CA: Pfeifferand Company, 1992.

Hawawini, G., Subramanian, V. and Verdin, P., 'Is Performance Driven by Industry- or Firm-specific Factors? A New Look at the Evidence', *Strategic Management Journal* 24(1) (2003), pp. 1-16.

Hofstede, Geert, *Culture's Consequences: International Differences in Work-related Values.* Thousand Oaks, CA: Sage Publications, 2001.

Ibn Taymiyyah, *Al-Siyasat al-Shari`ah fi Islah al-Ra'i wa Ra'iyyah (On Public and Private Law in Islam).* Beirut, Lebanon: Khayats, 1966.

Institute for Social Policy and Understanding, *Enhancing Board Performance in the Islamic Nonprofit Sector,* 2005.

Iqbal, M., *Khizr-E-Raah.* Translated by Tariq and Aziz. Lahore, Pakistan: Pan Islamic Publications. n.d.

ISL Software, *Winalim.* Silver Springs, MD: ISL Software Corporation, 1996, Release 4.

Jabnoun, N., *Islam and Management.* Riyadh, Saudi Arabia: International Islamic Publishing House, 2001.

Janis, I., *Victims of Groupthink: A Psychological Study of Foreign Policy Decisions and Fiascos.* Boston, Mass: Houghton Mifflin, 1973.

Kelleher, H., *Nuts! Southwest Airlines' Crazy Recipe for Business and Personal Success.* Austin, TX: Bard Press, 1996.

Khan, W., *Muhammad: A Prophet for Humanity.* New Delhi, India: Goodword Books, 1998.

Kotler, P., *Marketing Management: Analysis, Planning and Control.* Upper Saddle River, NJ: Prentice-Hall, 2005.

Kotter, J. P., *A Force for Change: How Leadership Differs from Management.* New York, NY: Free Press, 1990.

Kouzes, J. M. and Posner, B. Z., *The Leadership Challenge.* San Francisco, CA: Jossey-Bass, 1995.

BIBLIOGRAPHY

Kutty, A., 'Fatwa', Online at www.Islamonline.net, 2002.

Lawler, E. A., Finegold, D. L., Benson, G. S. and Conger, J. A., 'Corporate Boards: Keys to Effectiveness', *Organizational Dynamics* 30(4) (2002), pp. 310-324.

Legislative Budget Bureau, *Instructions for Preparing and Submitting Agency Strategic Plans*. Austin, TX: Governor's Office of Budget, Planning and Policy, 2004.

Levitt, T., 'Marketing Myopia', *Harvard Business Review* (July-August 1960), pp. 45-56.

Lings, M., *Muhammad: His Life Based on the Earliest Sources*. Rochester, VT: Inner Traditions, 1983.

March, J and Simon, H., *Organizations*. New York: Wiley, 1958.

Marcus, A., *Management Strategy: Sustaining Competitive Advantage*, Burr Ridge, IL: McGraw Hill/Irwin, 2005.

Marshall, M., 'Is Strategic Planning Biblical? Looking at leaders from Scripture', *Church Administration*, (Fall 2002).

McNamara, Carter. *Field Guide to Nonprofit Strategic Planning and Facilitation*. Minneapolis, Minnesota, 2003.

Migliore, R. H., Stevens, R. E., Loudon, D. L., and Williamson, S., *Strategic Planning for Not-for-Profit Organizations*. NY: Binghamton, The Haworth Press, 1995.

Mintzberg, H., *Structure in Fives: Designing Effective Organizations*. Upper Saddle River, NJ: Prentice-Hall, 1983

Morrisey, G. L., *A Guide to Tactical Planning*. San Francisco, CA: Jossey-Bass, 1996.

Mujahid, A. M., 'Tawakkul', Reprinted with permission from www.soundvision.com, 2005.

An-Nawawi, *Hadith Qudsi*. Beirut, Lebanon: The Holy Qur'an Publishing House, 1979.

Patton, G., "Quotations." www.generalpatton.com.

Pearce, J. A. and Zahra, S. A., 'The Relative Power of CEOs and Boards of Directors: Associations with Corporate Performance', *Strategic Management Journal* 12(2) (1991), pp. 135-153.

Perrow, C., *Organizational Analysis: A Sociological View*. Belmont, CA: Wadsworth Publishing Co., 1970.

Peters, T. and Waterman, R., *In Search of Excellence*. New York, NY: Harper & Row, 1982.

Phillips, R., *Stakeholder Theory and Organizational Ethics*. San Francisco, CA: Berrett Koehler, 2003.

Porter, M. E., *Competitive Strategy: Techniques for Analyzing Industries and Competitors*. New York, NY: Free Press, 1980.

Porter, M. E., *Competitive Advantage*. New York, NY: Free Press, 1995.

Puffer, S., 'Global Executive: Intel's Andrew Grove on Competitiveness', *Academy of Management Executive* 13(1) (February 1999), pp. 15-24.

Al-Qaradawi, Yusuf. *Al-Halal wa al-Haram fi al-Islam*. Indianapolis: American Trust Publications. n.d.

Al-Qaradawi, Yusuf, *Dawr al-Qiyam wa al-Akhlaq fi al-Iqtisad al-Islami*. Maktabat Wahbah, 1995.

Quinn, James B., *Strategies for Change: Logical Incrementalism*. Homewood, IL: Irwin, 1980.

Qutb, S., *Social Justice in Islam*. New York: Octagon Books, 1980.

Ringland, G., *Scenarios in Business*. West Sussex, UK: Wiley, 2002.

Rosly, S. A., 'The Inseparable *Shar`i* and *Tabi`* Principles in Business Strategy', 2004, www.dinarstandard.com.

Rost, J. C., *Leadership for the Twenty-first Century*. New York, NY: Praeger, 1991.

Saeed, M., Ahmed, Z. U and Mukhtar, S., 'International Marketing Ethics from an Islamic Perspective: A Value-maximization Approach', *Journal of Business Ethics* 32 (2001), 127-42.

Savola Group, 'Winning in the MENA Region and Beyond.' 2005 www.savola.com.

Schein, E. H., *Organizational Culture and Leadership*, 2nd. edn. San Francisco, CA: Jossey-Bass, 1997.

Schwartz, P., *The Art of the Long View*. New York, NY: Doubleday, 1997.

Shikoh, Rafi-uddin, 'Savola Group's Balanced Way: A Sure Ingredient for Sustained Growth', October 1, 2004 www.dinarstandard.com, Reprinted with permission.

Siddiqui, Ataullah, 'Ethics in Islam: Key Concepts and Contemporary Challenges', *Journal of Moral Education* 26(4) (1997), pp. 423-32.

Siddiqui, A. H., *Sahih Muslim* (n.p.: n.d.), volume 3.

Spulber, D. F., *Management Strategy*. Burr Ridge, IL: McGraw-Hill/Irwin, 2004.

Thomas, P. R., *Total Cycle Time: An Overview for CEOs*. New York, NY: McGraw-Hill, 1990.

Thompson, A., Jr., Gamble, J. E., and Strickland, A. J., *Strategy: Core Concepts, Analytical Tools and Readings*. New York, NY: McGraw-Hill/Irwin, 2005.

Tregoe, B. B., Zimmerman, J. W., Smith, R. A., and Tobia, P. M., *Vision in Action*. New York, NY: Simon and Schuster, 1989.

'Umar-ud-din, Muhammad, *The Ethical Philosophy of Al-Ghazzali*. Lahore, Pakistan, Sh. Muhammad Ashraf, 1991.

Weick, K., *The Social Psychology of Organizing*. Reading, MA: Addison Wesley, 1979.

Wiggins, R. and Ruefli, T., 'Sustained Competitive Advantage: Temporal Dynamics and the Incidence and Persistence of Superior Economic Performance', *Organization Science* 13(1) (2002), pp. 82-107.

INDEX

A

Abraham, 99, 153, 154, 187
Abu Bakr, 51, 90, 126, 155,187
Adalah, 4
Adaptability, 72, 73
Adaptation, 72, 73
Adl, 118, 147, 185
Akhirah, 4, 185
Ali, 47, 97, 99, 100, 126, 192, 194, 200
Al-Qaradawi, Yusuf, 189, 196
Amanah, 55, 68, 124, 126, 148
Animals, 2, 196
'Aql, 5
'Asabiyyah, 8, 9, 15, 45, 185
'Azm, 32, 124, 185

B

Badr, 3
Board of Directors, 15, 19, 22, 23, 27, 47, 138, 142, 151

C

CAIR, 8, 29, 30,44, 50, 51, 53, 56, 91, 92, 120, 137
Change process, 18, 22
Charity, 50, 119, 146
Closed system, 46
Collaborator Analysis, 36
Commitment, 11, 16, 18, 19, 21, 42, 45, 48, 55, 99, 100, 102, 124, 126, 194, 199
Competencies, 9, 23, 28, 29, 30, 33, 36, 48, 50, 52, 65-68, 93, 116, 127, 199, 200

Competitor analysis, 37, 38, 39, 170
Contingency Plan, 87-89, 93, 95
Corporate Character Theory, 151
Covey, 48, 192, 200
Cultural Audit, 32
Cultural
    Assumptions, 32, 37, 117, 119-122
    Definition, 117
    Model, 119, 120
    Values, 16, 29, 32, 48, 54-57, 117-122
Curse of competence, 28, 29, 47

D

David, 2, 123
Decision making, 125, 188
Dhat al-Salasil, Battle of, 81
Driving forces, 39, 40, 91,92

E

Egocentricism, 45, 46
Ethical values, 53, 118, 146
Expertise, 13, 17, 27, 45, 81, 111., 130, 181

F

Feedback, xi, 19, 47, 92, 96, 102, 131, 133, 137
Fit, 27, 70, 72, 73, 74, 78, 89, 95, 96, 105, 106, 110, 112, 117, 127, 141, 142, 174, 175, 190, 191
Functional area plans, 82

G

Goal, 2,11,36, 47, 60, 64, 67, 75-77, 83, 84, 115, 130, 133, 135, 174-176, 178, 181, 182
Green dot balloting, 34, 60
Groupthink, 17, 36, 46, 47, 60, 190-192, 201

H

Halal, 4, 5, 7, 57, 68, 145, 146, 186, 199
Haram, 4, 145, 146, 186, 196, 199
Hijrah, 68, 186
Hudaybiyyah, 3, 64, 65

I

Ibn al-Yaman, Hudhayfah, 25, 26
Ibn Taymiyyah, 81, 190, 201
ICLI, 180-183, 198
Ihsan, 4, 7, 8, 32, 48, 118, 148, 149, 186
Ihsan al-Dhan, 32, 125
Iman, 5, 122, 154, 186
IMRC, 8, 29, 50, 51, 61, 72, 77, 83, 120
Intention, 20, 100, 122, 144, 152, 184, 187
Iqtida, 32, 124
ISNA, 8, 28, 53, 77, 139
Itqan, 32, 124

J

Jerusalem, 97, 121, 183
Jesus, 99
Joseph, 2, 3, 104
Justice, 4, 43, 44, 53, 54, 56, 120, 124, 144, 147, 151, 185, 197, 203

K

Khalid ibn Walid, 20, 37, 73, 87, 139
Khandaq, 4, 41, 42, 70
King (Jr.), Martin Luther, 43

L

Leadership
    Five-step model, 96
    Transformational, 97, 101

M

Medina, 26
Mission statement, 11, 41, 43, 44, 48, 49, 51, 52, 54, 57, 99, 126, 171, 172, 191, 192, 199
Moses, 2, 3, 99, 105
MSA, 8
Mu`azarah, 125
Muhammad, viii, xi, 3, 8, 9, 41, 51, 54, 64, 70, 90, 97-99, 100, 102, 103, 143, 144, 154, 155, 183, 186, 187, 189-191, 193, 201-203
munafasah, 67

N

Noah, 2, 99

O

Objectives, 10, 11, 37-39, 75, 76, 77, 78, 82, 83, 88, 96, 101, 129, 132-136, 138, 142, 154, 167, 176, 181

P

Pareto Rule, 60
Patriot Act, 22, 40, 91
Performance
    Evaluation & review, 129-131, 142, 194, 199
    Measure, 132, 134, 135
Performance gap, 64, 132
Pledge (the), 20, 26, 148
Pre-planning, 15

Q

Qist, 147

Qur'an, 1-4, 7, 8, 40, 41, 49, 54, 63, 95, 103, 104, 118, 121, 122, 141, 143, 144, 147, 148, 150-155, 157, 158, 180, 183, 185-189

Qutb, Syed, 99, 150, 197, 203

R

Responsibility, xi, 20, 22, 26, 55, 57, 83, 86, 93, 101, 124, 134, 146-152, 157, 195-197, 199

S

Savola, 29, 32, 44, 52, 56, 123-126, 130, 131, 195, 196, 203

Scenario Building, 88, 90, 91

Sirah, xi, 2, 8, 25, 118, 155, 188, 190

Shar`i* and *Tabi` principles, 4, 5, 189, 203

Shar`i* and *Tabi` principles of strategy, 4–7

Shar`i, 4, 5, 189, 203

Shura, 7, 15, 22, 27, 28, 45, 46, 47, 81, 82, 93, 98, 99, 133, 138

Skills, 27, 28, 77, 81, 83, 98, 115

SMART criteria, 75, 78

Stakeholder, 12, 15, 17, 18, 27, 122, 136, 146, 164, 174, 190, 197, 200, 202

Statement of philosophy, 54, 55, 173, 174, 175

Strategic management, 1-13
    Fallacy of detachment, 12
    Fallacy of formalization, 12
    Fallacy of prediction, 13
    Pitfalls, 12
    Strategy formulation,
    Strategy Implementation, 5, 7, 9, 10, 22, 60, 63, 81, 96, 97, 126, 142

Strategic myopia, 49, 101

Strategic planning, xi, 1, 2, 3, 5, 6, 9, 10, 12, 13, 15, 16, 19-21, 41, 131, 137, 147, 154, 155, 163, 164, 165, 170, 177, 189, 190, 192, 193, 196, 199-202

Strategic Planning Committee, 12, 16, 17, 164, 165

Structure
    Contingency approach, 107
    Definition, 107
    Divisional, 110-114
    Dynamic network, 109, 116
    Functional, 109, 112, 114
    Geographical, 111, 112
    Hybrid, 112, 113
    Matrix, 113-115

Sultan Fateh, 68

Sustainable competitive advantage, 4, 67, 73, 74

SWOT, 10, 25-27, 31-33, 34, 39, 46, 48, 59, 63, 65, 88, 89, 142, 166-169

T

Tabi`*. See *Shar`i and *Tabi`* principles

Tabi`, 4, 5, 203

Targets, xi, 10, 39, 73, 82, 83, 86, 104, 170, 183

Tawadu', 32

Tawakkul, 13, 154, 156, 157, 158, 197

U

Uhud, 87, 88, 102

Umar, 47, 67, 81, 97, 99, 121, 126, 139, 144, 151, 154

Ummah, 41, 42, 46, 139, 185, 188

V

Value chain, 50, 51, 109
Value-maximization, 27, 193, 203
Vision, 7, 10, 11, 28, 41, 42-48, 54, 57, 63, 77, 83, 85, 88, 99, 100, 103, 124, 126, 127, 132, 137, 138, 142, 165, 167, 171, 172, 174, 175, 179, 180, 184, 203
Vision statement, 11, 41-43, 46, 48, 77, 171

W

Worship, 10, 61, 122, 147, 152, 187, 198

X

X, Malcolm, 97, 99

AHMED O. LAMPTEY